EARLY SHIPS
AND
SEAFARING

EARLY SHIPS AND SEAFARING

European Water Transport

European Water Transport

Seán McGrail

First published in Great Britain in 2014 by
PEN AND SWORD ARCHAEOLOGY
an imprint of
Pen and Sword Books Ltd
47 Church Street
Barnsley
South Yorkshire S70 2AS

ISBN 978 1 78159 392 9

Printed and bound in England
by CPI Group (UK) Ltd, Croydon, CR0 4YY

Typeset in Times New Roman by
CHIC GRAPHICS

Pen & Sword Books Ltd incorporates the imprints of
Pen & Sword Books Ltd incorporates the imprints of Pen & Sword
Archaeology, Atlas, Aviation, Battleground, Discovery, Family
History, History, Maritime, Military, Naval, Politics, Railways, Select,
Social History, Transport, True Crime, Claymore Press, Frontline Books,
Leo Cooper, Praetorian Press, Remember When, Seaforth Publishing
and Wharncliffe..

For a complete list of Pen and Sword titles please contact
Pen and Sword Books Limited
47 Church Street, Barnsley, South Yorkshire, S70 2AS, England
E-mail: enquiries@pen-and-sword.co.uk
Website: www.pen-and-sword.co.uk

Contents

Preface

Two-thirds of the world's surface is covered by sea; the other third has numerous lakes and rivers which were pre-eminently early Man's 'highways'. Since the Stone Age, water transport on lake, river and sea has been the prime means by which Man explored and exploited the world, linked together its dispersed populations, and sustained trade and exchange. The raft and the boat (later the ship) remained principle actors in that role until the advent of the aeroplane in the early twentieth century.

Boats are their own advertisement: there therefore has been a tendency for styles of boat building and methods of propulsion and steering to spread around centres of innovation and become regional styles. The aim of this volume is to present what is now known about the water transport of two of those regions: the Mediterranean and the European Atlantic seaboard. The time span of the text extends from earliest days to the fifteenth century AD when European ships had begun to be designed in a formal way, and technical descriptions and drawings of water transport were produced.

A significant change in water transport occurred with the introduction of the ship – with all that increase in size implies for operational capabilities. In the English language, there is no clear dividing line between the two, merely a range of characteristics of which the ship, generally speaking, has more than the planked boat. The Oxford English Dictionary defines the 'boat' as 'a small open vessel; the 'ship' as 'a large seagoing vessel'. A distinction is thereby drawn between, on the one hand, a small, un-decked vessel ('the boat') limited in range and by the weather, and using informal landing places; and, on the other hand, a large, decked vessel ('the planked ship'), capable of carrying a boat onboard, relatively unrestricted in range or by the weather, and often operated from formal harbours with wharfs and jetties.

PREFACE

Large vessels that might well be called 'ships' seem to have been built in certain regions of the world after Iron Age technology (a necessary, but not sufficient condition) was acquired. Nevertheless, vessels of the medieval Nordic ('Viking') tradition that were sailed across the north Atlantic Ocean and might therefore, be considered 'ships' were, structurally, 'open boats'. Clearly there are nomenclature problems. In the chapters that follow I have attempted to distinguish between 'boats' and 'ships' but may not always have succeeded.

In earlier times (and still today, in places around the world) rafts and boats built of bark, logs, bundles and hides were not only relatively quickly built, but also matched both the role they were destined to undertake and the environment in which they were to be used. In the long run, however, it proved to be only the plank boat that could be increased in size to become the ship capable of sailing the oceans of the world.

In Chapter One, concepts and techniques are described that are used in the succeeding chapters. Of particular importance is the section dealing, in simple terms, with naval architectural concepts such as 'flotation and stability' and 'seaworthiness'. Chapters Two and Three deal with the Mediterranean and with Atlantic Europe, regions with distinctive cultural and technological histories. Those two chapters each begin with a description of the region's hydrography and maritime geography based, with permission, on a similar text published in Chapters Four and Five of my *Boats of the World* (2001, Oxford University Press). Those descriptions are followed by an exposition of the region's main traditions of float, raft and boat/ship building. The third element in each chapter is a description of how such water transport was used: propulsion, steering, navigation and the like, including (where the information is available) the identification of early harbours and landing places.

As the reader will find, there are great gaps in our knowledge, especially in the early times when reliance has to be placed almost entirely on excavated evidence, which is not only sparse but also incomplete. Moreover, on excavation, such remains are seldom found to be arranged in an orderly and readily-understood fashion, which may sometimes lead to doubt and disagreement about how they should be interpreted. Nevertheless, it is generally agreed that, for certain times and places – for example, the Eastern Mediterranean in the Classical and Byzantine periods, and in tenth to twelfth century AD Scandinavia – a reasonably coherent, moderately comprehensive, and probably fairly accurate picture can be presented. For other times and places, as orderly an account as possible has been given.

Chilmark
Feast of St Thomas Aquinas
2014

CHAPTER 1

Concepts and Techniques

In 1946, James Hornell, marine biologist by profession but nautical ethnographer-historian by inclination, published *Water Transport*, a remarkable volume that summarised his wide-ranging – almost worldwide – knowledge of working rafts and boats. In his preface, Hornell defined water transport as 'the many devices upon which men, living in varying stages of culture, launch themselves afloat upon river, lake and sea' Hornell's 'many devices' may be divided into four classes: floats, rafts, boats and ships. For reasons of brevity, the term 'ship' is used in the title of this book. Nevertheless, for our purposes here, ships may be thought of as large boats; the three other classes may be distinguished, one from another, by considering how the buoyancy of each is derived or applied.

<u>Floats</u> are personal aids to flotation: a float's buoyancy is applied direct to the man partly immersed in the water. Outside tropical waters, the seagoing use of floats is constrained by water temperature and limited by the endurance of the user.

<u>Rafts</u> derive their buoyancy from the flotation characteristics of each individual element which must have a specific density less than 1 (i.e. it must float). Some rafts are 'boat shaped', nevertheless they are 'flow-through' structures and are therefore not boats. Like floats, rafts are used on rivers and lakes but their 'flow-through' characteristic means that, outside the zones of warmer water (approximately 40°N to 40°S) their use at sea is limited and is, indeed, impossible when cold air and sea temperatures are combined with exposure to wind and/or rain to the point where the crew are disabled by hypothermia.

1

<u>Boats</u> derive their buoyancy from the flotation characteristics of a hollowed vessel as water is displaced by its watertight hull. There are no limitations on the specific density of hull materials, although those made of lighter materials will float higher in the water and therefore be able to carry greater loads.

Within these groups, sub-divisions may be recognised by reference to the principal raw material used. Thus there are log floats, hide floats, bundle floats and pot floats; rafts of logs, of inflated floats, of bundles and of pots; and boats of logs, bark, hides, pottery, reed bundles, coiled basketry (the latter two waterproofed by bitumen) and planks.

BOATBUILDING SEQUENCES

Several of those sub-types may be further partitioned depending on whether they are built as a watertight shell or as a waterproofed frame. Planked boats are either 'plank-first' ('shell-first' – Fig. 1.1) or 'frame-first' ('skeleton-first' – Fig. 1.2). In the former case, the watertight planking defines the shape of the hull which is subsequently strengthened by framing. In the second case the hull is defined by the framing which is subsequently made watertight by planking fastened to that framework.

Fig. 1.1 The plank-first sequence of building a boat. (after Crumlin-Pedersen)

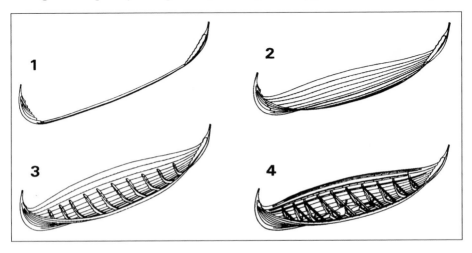

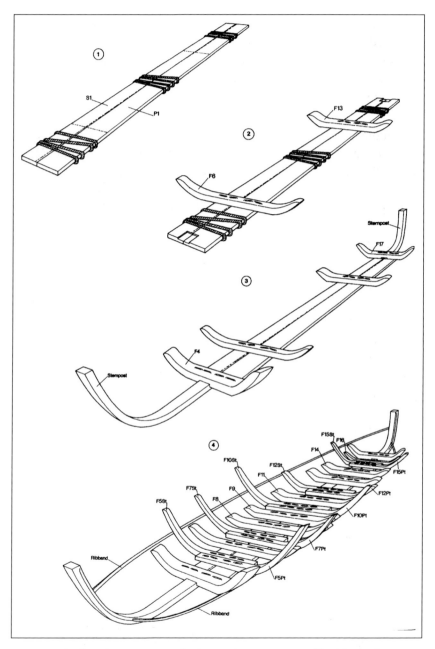

Fig. 1.2 The first four stages in the frame-first sequence of building a boat.

Logboats are built 'shell-first'. Bark boats are also generally built 'shell-first', but recently, in Sweden, British Columbia and Siberia, some (the larger ones?) were built by sewing or lashing bark pieces to a framework. Most hide boats are built skeleton-first; they are then made watertight by the addition of a hide cover. Small ('one-hide') boats in North America and in Mongolia, on the other hand, were built as a watertight shell (a 'leather bag') which was sometimes re-enforced by framing.

If hull planking is found fastened together (rather than to a framework) it is almost certain that such a vessel had been built in the 'shell' (plank-first) sequence. Exceptionally, however, there was a period in China (fourteenth to fifteenth centuries AD – and on to the twentieth century) when seagoing ships with planking fastened together had actually been built frame-first.

Although archaeologists identify these two different approaches to boatbuilding by determining the building sequence, early plank-boat builders would probably have thought of them as different ways of obtaining hull shape. In the plank-first case, shape was determined by eye, and visualised as a watertight shell of planking reinforced by framing. In frame-first building, on the other hand, shape was obtained by fashioning individual frames and setting them so that the required hull shape was outlined: such boats were visualised as a framework skeleton that was subsequently 'waterproofed' by planking.

BOATBUILDING TRADITIONS

A ship- or boat-building tradition is an archaeological concept; it may be defined as 'the perceived style of building generally used in a region during a given time range'. Such traditions were initially recognised by archaeologists using intuitive, ad hoc methods. As more wrecks were found, it proved possible to identify characteristics that seemed to define certain groups. An important, often diagnostic, feature is the type of fastening used in a boat, either to fasten planking together or to fasten planking to framework (Figs. 1.3 & 1.4).

Fig. 1.3 European fastenings.

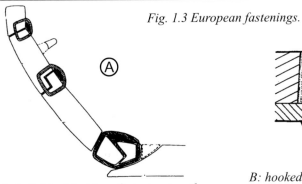

A: *individual lashings fastening together the planking of the Ferriby boats.*

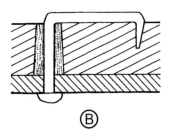

B: *hooked nails fastening the planking to the framing of Romano-Celtic vessels.*

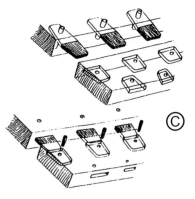

C: *locked mortise and tenon plank fastenings of early-Mediterranean vessels.*

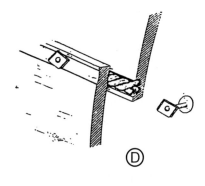

D: *clenched iron nails fastening together the hair-caulked, overlapping planking of Nordic vessels*

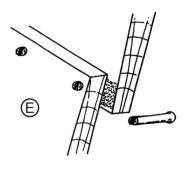

E: *Slavonic variant of 'D', with moss caulking and treenail fastenings.*

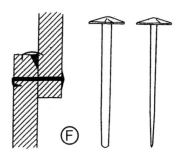

F: *Hooked nails fastening together the clinker planking of the Bremen Cog, with moss caulking held in place by metal clamps.*

Fig. 1.4. Plank fastenings used in India, Vietnam, China & the South Pacific.

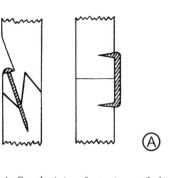

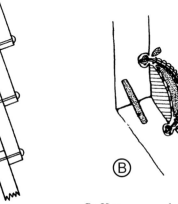

A: South-Asian fastenings: (left) angled nails (vadhera) in Gujarat; (centre) staples in Bangladesh; (right) reverse-clinker planking (outboard is to the left) fastened with hooked nails in Orissa and West Bengal.

B: Vietnamese planking positioned by wooden dowels, and fastened together by wedged rattan lashings.

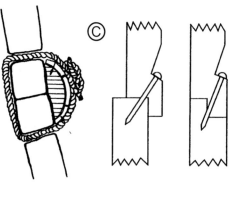

C: Chinese fastenings: coir lashings of a boat from Hainan island (left); and two types of angled–nail fastening in Quanzhou ship 1.

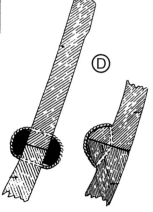

D: Maori (left) and Fijian sewn-plank methods of fastening planking to a logboat hull using coconut-fibre cord over a caulking.

The Nordic building tradition (Ch. 3) originated in the western Baltic in the early centuries AD and reached its climax during Viking times (eighth to eleventh centuries AD): some of its features continued to be recognisable in wrecks and illustrations dated as late as the fourteenth century. Other traditions had been given type names during late-medieval times: 'cog', 'hulc' and 'carrack', for example. Contemporary illustrations and descriptions allow us to link some of these type-names with excavated wrecks – there is now a sizeable group of vessels recognised as cogs. Other evident traditions, for which no type name has survived, have to be given a name: for example, the term, 'Romano-Celtic' is used to describe a group of second to fourth centuries AD, north-west European vessels (some seagoing, others river craft), with several characteristics in common.

It is not necessary that all vessels thought to be of one tradition should possess all characteristics. Each vessel in a tradition has to share a large number of characteristics with all others, but no one characteristic has to be possessed by all of them. Such groups are said to be 'polythetic', and, in not requiring uniformity, they reflect our intuitive understanding of the real world.

BOATBUILDING MATERIAL & TOOLS
Hides, reeds, and other materials – even pottery – have been used to build boats but, worldwide, timber is especially important, being the principal material for log rafts, log boats, and (pre-eminently) planked boats. Wood is also used for the framework of buoyed rafts, hide boats and reed-bundle boats, and for the lashings and sewing used to fasten together sewn-plank boats, hide boats and bundle rafts. Furthermore, wooden pegs (treenails) have been used widely to fasten planking together and to secure fittings, such as frames, to boats. Moreover, bark – another tree product – is used to build bark boats and some bundle rafts. The dominance of the tree in early boatbuilding was emphasised by G.F. Hourani, in his mid-twentieth century book on 'Arab Seafaring': he noted that a traditional Arab sewn-plank boat could be made solely from a coconut tree: planking, mast and other fittings from the bole, ropes, plank fastenings and

sails from coir (the fibrous husk of the nut), and waterproofing oil from dried nut kernels.

In north-west Europe, ash, elm, hazel, alder, beech yew, lime, birch, willow and pine were sometimes used in boatbuilding but, wherever oak was available, it was clearly preferred for the main structural elements. Individual trees were carefully selected to match each job in hand: tall forest oaks with straight grain and without low branches had boles that were suitable for logboats, for long, straight, almost knot-free planks, and for keels and keelsons. Isolated oaks, on the other hand, produced naturally-curved timber that was needed for tholes, knees, frames, stems and other curved members (Fig. 1.5).

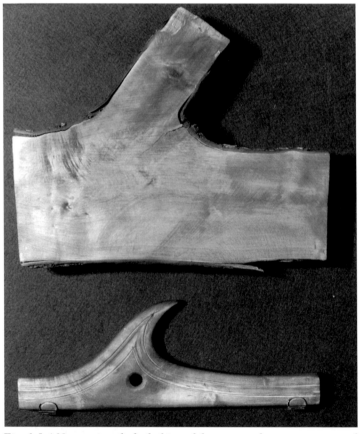

Fig. 1.5 A Norwegian thole fashioned from a crook to ensure strength.

Archaeological and historical evidence, and recent practice in Shetland and Norway, suggest that early boats were built of 'green' timber, unseasoned and therefore of relatively high moisture content. Such 'green' timber was easier to work, and the tendency for it to split and distort was minimised. The finished boat was then stabilised in a similarly high moisture content environment by transferring it to its natural habitat, the sea.

After the crown and major branches had been removed from a felled tree, the resultant log was stripped of its bark and sapwood. From such a log, or sometimes a half log, logboats were hollowed out. Whole, straight logs were also converted into keels for planked boats. In prehistoric times, whole or half-log oaks were converted into planks, thus achieving the maximum plank breadth from near the diameter of the log; in medieval times pine logs (of smaller diameter than oak) were similarly converted. Oak planks for medieval boats

Fig. 1.6 Diagram showing two ways of converting logs into planks:

Oak: An Oak log was converted into radial planks by first splitting the log in half; then halving each of those halves; and so on.
Pine: Pine logs (of smaller diameter) could best be converted into two planks, one from each half.
The lower diagram shows how a plank orientated radially in its parent oak log has rays running the breadth of the plank (a) and therefore will be strong; a plank orientated tangentially (b) would be less-strong.

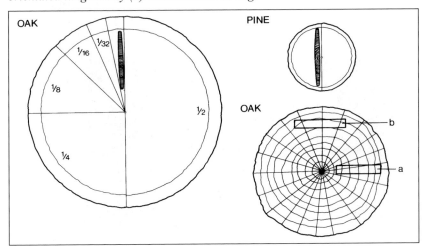

built in the Nordic ('Viking') tradition were split radially from oak logs (Fig. 1.6). Such 'clove boards' are stronger than planks converted in any other way; they shrink less in breadth, are less liable to split or warp, and are less easily penetrated by fungi. Splitting radially also minimises the number of planks with knots in them, and the wedge-shaped cross sections of each plank admirably fit the overlap, a distinctive feature of clinker planking.

Nowadays, an experienced forester would expect to produce twenty sound, radial planks per log; in medieval times, more may have been achieved. This method of log conversion persisted in north-west Europe until the fourteenth century when saws began to be used for shipbuilding and it became possible to convert logs in a variety of ways. Saws generally follow a straight line, regardless of the grain, whereas radially splitting an oak log, using beech or metal wedges, follows natural lines of cleavage ('grain') and the boards thus produced are stronger than sawn boards.

In Britain, the individual stitches used to fasten together the planks of the Earlier Bronze Age Ferriby boats were made from un-split yew withies, twisted and cracked to make them flexible. The continuous, sewn fastenings of the Brigg 'raft', of the Later Bronze Age, consisted of two, inter-twinned, split strands of poplar/willow. Two-stranded birch rope was used to repair a split in the Appleby logboat of *c.*1100 BC. By late-medieval times rigging ropes were much as we know them today: at Wood Quay in Dublin, ten to fifteen yarns of split or whole yew withies were bundled into strands, and two strands were then laid up right-handed to make a rope of some four inches girth.

Boats can be built with a relatively simple tool kit: the Nootka Indians of America's west coast used bird bones to bore holes, and the Chumash Indians of California used flints and whalebone wedges to build seagoing, sewn-plank boats. In early-twentieth century Oceania, boats were built with stone and bone tools. Elsewhere, shells were used for tasks that, today, we would use axe, adze or scraper. In early technologies everywhere, a simple kit of non-metal tools was used to build, what excavation shows to have been, splendid examples of the boatbuilder's art.

In the absence of wind-uprooted trees or of driftwood, living trees must be prepared for felling by lopping-off branches using stone or (later) metal, axes. Maori woodsmen felled totara pine trees using stone tools and a ballista-powered, or swing, battering ram to cut into a tree's base. There is also much ethnographic evidence for the controlled use of fire. The crown and any remaining limbs were removed, and wedges, levers, ropes and rollers used to manoeuvre the resulting log into a position where it could be converted. Bark and sapwood were then removed and surplus timber cut away to produce something near the final shape required.

When planks were to be fashioned in northern Europe, oak logs were split by wedge, mallet and lever, until pitsaws and sawmills become common in the later middle ages. A plank was fashioned from each half of a split pine log, thus obtaining maximum plank breadth. Certain timber species may be bent without treatment; other species after being made malleable by controlled burning or by steam. Ropes, wedges and levers may also be used. Planks may be held together temporarily by a simple tourniquet or by X-shaped, wooden cramps, locked by a wedge. Much was done 'by eye', based on years of experience, or using natural measurement units such as thumbs, palm,

Fig. 1.7. Boatbuilding scene from the Bayeux tapestry. (Photo: courtesy of the Muséé de l'Evêché. Bayeux.)

hand-spans, feet, ells and fathoms. On some excavated, medieval boats, knives, or scribing tools, had been used to 'mark-off' the intended position for the next timber. Axes could have been used to fashion most shapes required in boat building (Fig. 1.7), except where very concave shapes were needed, as in the underside of some frames, hollowed garboards and hollowed stems: in those cases, adze, chisel or knife would have been used.

In Britain, fastening holes in the Bronze Age Ferriby sewn-plank boats were worked by chisel or gouge; 1,000 years later, holes in the Brigg 'raft' were probably bored by a bow-drill or by leather thong. Other tools needed when sewing together the planks of these early boats included a blade to split the willow withy used as thread, and a tensioning tool to tighten the thread before it was wedged in position. Holes for fastenings in medieval times may have been bored by hot metal or by awl, gimlet or auger (depicted on the Bayeux tapestry – Fig. 1.7).

Saws became available in north-west Europe during Roman times and were used, for example, to fashion the planks of Romano-Celtic boats (see Ch. 3, p.124–134). They were not used there again for boatbuilding until the thirteenth/fourteenth century AD. In the Mediterranean, saws were used when building the fourth century BC Kyrenia ship (see p.80–81).

SOURCES OF EVIDENCE

During the past 100 years or so, within the coastal waters and rivers of lands bordering the European Atlantic, the Baltic and the Mediterranean, a number of ancient vessels have been discovered, excavated, researched and published. In recent years, several medieval wrecks from Chinese and south-east Asian waters have similarly been published. Elsewhere in the world, however, such projects are exceptional. Even within Europe, there are no excavated boats dated earlier than the eighth millennium BC: the oldest is a logboat; and the oldest European plank boat is from the early-second millennium BC.

Iconographic, documentary and ethnographic data can be used to supplement data derived from excavation and also to tell us something about water transport in periods when there are few, if any, excavated vessels.

CONCEPTS AND TECHNIQUES

Iconographic evidence

In India, representations of boats are the earliest and, indeed, the only evidence for water transport until the sixteenth century when written accounts by European travellers begin to appear. Moreover, worldwide, sails and rigging rarely survive to be excavated, so depictions on stones, engravings on seals and pottery decorations can clarify our ideas about propulsion. Models of boats can be especially rewarding since the vessel's cross section, unseen on two-dimensional depictions, can provide an indication of the uses and the capabilities of the vessel represented.

Depiction and models should be accepted only after a rigorous assessment. Even when agreement is reached on the identification of bow and stern, and on the scale the original artist probably used, disagreement can remain about precise interpretation: see, for example, the several, very different interpretations of the shape and size of the central boat depicted on the Bronze Age Thera frieze (see p.64–65). Furthermore, it must be remembered that such representations were not produced by twentieth century naval architects, but by ancient craftsmen who may have had only an indifferent knowledge of nautical matters.

One research method that can prove fruitful is to investigate the artistic conventions used within different cultures. For example, vertical lines across a 'hull' in an Arabian context probably represent the bindings of a bundle raft, whereas, horizontal lines may well indicate a planked boat. In representations from early Scandinavia, vertical lines above a hull may indicate members of the crew; in contrast, vertical lines extending below the hull may represent paddles or oars.

Documentary evidence

Documentary evidence can range widely, from ancient inscriptions and law codes to comprehensive, illustrated reports on vessels published by recent explorers and travellers. Those later accounts were compiled with the aim of passing on specialist knowledge; earlier accounts only rarely had this objective in mind, rather they mention, in passing, some minor aspect of boat building, appearance or use, within a text principally concerned with an un-related topic. Nevertheless, such is the paucity of evidence about earlier, and even recent, water transport in most parts of the world, that such scraps of evidence are important.

To ensure that reliable information about the past is obtained from these descriptions, it is necessary to determine the standpoint and the nautical competence of the narrator, and the provenance in time and space of each document has to be established. As with iconographic evidence, documentary evidence of water transport is unlikely to be unbiased and, while objects and events that are commonplace to the observer are liable to be noted briefly, if at all, the unusual, which may not be representative of its time and place, may be described in detail.

Ethnographic evidence

'First contact' reports by fifteenth to eighteenth century European seamen concerning water transport encountered in America, Australia and the South Pacific are valuable since they were documented before European technologies had had any influence, by men who were familiar with nautical matters. When there is a clear link within a particular technological culture between the remote and the recent past, descriptions of recent tools and techniques used by builders of simple boats and rafts can make an archaeologist aware of a range of solutions to boat building and boat-use problems. Such awareness enables the archaeologist to escape constraints imposed by his own culture, and may well allow him to come closer to understanding the early technology being investigated.

There are problems in using cross-cultural comparisons in this way, but the more alike in environmental, technological and economic terms two cultures (one ancient, one modern) can be shown to be, the more likely it is that ethnographic data will be relevant to the investigation of ancient nautical technology and boat use. There is not necessarily a one-to-one relationship between an ancient boat (incomplete, fragmented and distorted) and an ethnographic boat. It is rather that ethnographic evidence can suggest the sort of questions to be asked of the ancient boat, and may also prompt a range of answers.

Nevertheless, as Professor Grahame Clark of Cambridge University said, over fifty years ago, "only archaeology, in conjunction with the various natural sciences, can give the right answers" – with a rider that, in the present state of learning, no answer may be possible, and that any answer will be probabilistic rather than definitive.

Dating

Excavated vessels do not always have datable artefacts directly associated with them therefore, until late in the twentieth century, boat remains were often dated by reference to the archaeological context in which they lay. In recent years, direct dating of a boat's timber has been possible using radiocarbon assay and, latterly, by dendrochronology with even greater precision. Vessels not dated by one of these direct methods should be considered merely provisionally dated.

Environmental evidence

In order to understand the problems and hazards faced by ancient mariners, it is necessary to construct a picture of the maritime environment that they faced. Things have not always been as they are now: there have been short term and long term climatic changes and, during the past 18,000 years, mean sea level worldwide has generally risen. It follows that, before we can investigate how Greater Australia or the Americas were first settled, mean sea level during the likely period of those settlements has to be established since it defines the lengths, and the number, of sea passages that such early migrants would have had to transit. Moreover, in conjunction with other factors, mean sea level determines, at a given time and place:

- The general form of the coastline which, in turn, influences local tidal regimes.
- River gradients, hence rates of erosion and deposition.
- The presence or absence of archipelagos, shoals, sands, skerries, tidal races, spits and bars.

The reconstruction of earlier coastlines, river channels and earlier weather patterns is complex since the effects of several interacting variables have to be estimated. Maps of several regions of the world, showing sea levels and coastlines, have been published: in the present state of research these are considered as a general guide rather than definitive.

Weather data from earlier times is either derived from dendrology and similar palaeo-research and is therefore generalized, or is based on averages and extrapolations of observations made in past centuries. As with coastlines, conclusions drawn about earlier weather and, indeed climate have to be stated in terms of probabilities.

NAVAL ARCHITECTURE

In order to appreciate the ancient boatbuilder's approach to his trade and thus gain insight from an examination of an excavated boat, it is necessary to understand the relationships between a boat's shape and structure, and the static and dynamic forces to which it is subjected when afloat. This is not to claim that the ancient boatbuilder based his art on scientific principles; rather that, over time, he empirically evolved techniques that enabled him to incorporate desired qualities in his boats. Naval architects nowadays know how to design the shape of a hull so that a vessel will have certain characteristics (speed, stability, cargo capacity, manoeuvrability etc). Nevertheless, since those characteristics are not independent variables, in practice, every vessel is a compromise. By studying the reconstructed hull of the vessel excavated, in a reversal of that process, maritime archaeologists with an understanding of basic naval architecture should be in a sound position to understand the qualities that her builder aimed to incorporate.

Formulae and diagrams do not appear to have been used by boatbuilders to produce hull shapes until the fifteenth century, and a craft approach to ship design prevailed in European shipyards until the seventeenth century when the first known calculations were made from which draft and displacement could be estimated and thus predictions of performance attempted. The theoretical problems to be solved in such a process are not simple, not least because water transport is used at the interface of two media: air and water. The motion of a sailing boat in a seaway is complex, and understanding that process remains as much an art as a science. In order to discuss such matters with a naval architect, and get an idea of an excavated craft's potential performance, maritime archaeologists need to be aware of this complexity.

Flotation and Stability

When a body is immersed, or partly-immersed, in water, Archimedes' principle states that it experiences an up-thrust (buoyancy) that equals the weight of the water displaced. In equilibrium, this buoyancy acts vertically upwards through (B), the centre of buoyancy (centroid) of the body (Fig. 1.8). In this state, the centre of mass (G) of the body will be on a line through (B). Furthermore, the weight of the water displaced by this body equals that of the body itself.

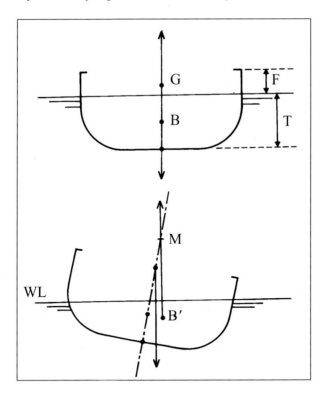

Fig. 1.8 Diagram illustrating transverse stability. When a hull is displaced from the vertical, the new buoyancy force (B'), acting through (M), returns the hull to the upright position. F=freeboard, T=draft, WL=waterline.

The volume of water displaced (V) equals the volume of the immersed part of the boat i.e. that below the waterline (WL), the position of which changes as the load carried is varied. The vertical distance from the waterline to the underside of the keel is known as the draft (T); the distance from this waterline to the top of the boat's side amidships is known as the freeboard (F) and is some measure of the boat's seaworthiness.

After the original form, structure, propulsion and steering of an excavated vessel have been theoretically re-constructed (p.41–42), the weight of the vessel, with and without loads, and the position of (G) in various load states is calculated using data from the reconstruction drawing. The centre of buoyancy (B) is obtained in a similar manner, estimating underwater areas (and thus weights) in all three planes by counting squares on a gridded drawing, or by using Simpsons's or Tchebycheff's rules. The longitudinal and transverse positions of (B) are thus obtained. (B), like (G), lies in the fore-and-aft middle plane, generally near the midships section.

Hydrostatic curves (Fig. 1.9)
For selected water planes (i.e. drafts) the weight of displaced water is calculated and the related displacement curve is plotted (displacement against draft). From such curves, the freeboard and draft for any specified loaded state may be obtained. Further curves may be obtained from the hull shape: tons per inch immersion; longitudinal centre of buoyancy (and of flotation); moment to change trim; the height of the centre of buoyancy (KB) and of the metacentre (GM). That 'mystic' point, the metacentre (M), is shown on Fig.1.8: its height (KM) above the keel is determined solely by the underwater shape of the hull. Providing (M) is higher than (G), when a boat is displaced from an upright position, the new buoyancy force, acting through (M), corrects this displacement. The distance (GM) (metacentric height) is a measure of the size of this righting moment. A boat with a large (GM) is said to be 'stiff'', and a vessel's motion may become unbearable; a small (GM) means a weak righting moment and the vessel is said to be 'tender' or 'crank': such vessels will be slow to return upright and

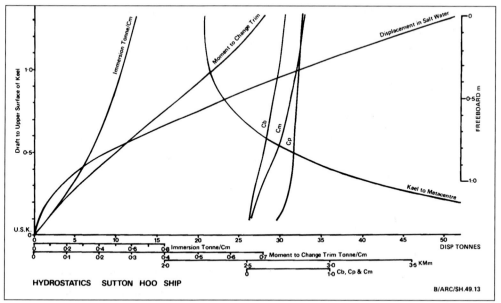

Fig. 1.9 Hydrostatic curves calculated from a reconstruction drawing of Sutton Hoo ship1.

may become unstable at large angles of heel. This all-important, metacentric height may be increased by:

(i). Lowering (G): Keep (G) low during building.
Cargo & passengers loaded low down; add ballast.
(ii).Increasing (BM): At constant displacement, stability varies as the cube of the waterline breadth (B^3).
At constant draft, stability varies as (B^2).

Thus, in general, the broader the waterline beam, the more stable the boat. Some measure of this is given by the coefficient B/T (where T = draft). A relatively deep vessel (low B/T) will have a small (BM), hence a small (GM) and thus be tender; examples of this were the notorious, early nineteenth century 'coffin ships'.

Without understanding the concept of metacentric height, negative stability can be recognised since, after heeling over, the boat stays there in a state of 'loll'. In former times, this state would have been avoided, leading to the evolution of hull shapes and loading methods that resulted in metacentric heights that were greater than the bare minimum and thus would have been noticeable in the greater righting moment induced.

Seaworthiness

A boat of the usual shape (broadest amidships, pointed bow and rounded stern) in the still waters of the proverbial mill-pond is subjected to varying stresses along its length. This is because there is an excess of buoyancy amidships, a deficiency at the stern, and an even greater deficiency at the bow. This imposed stress will tend to cause both ends of the vessel to droop – an effect known as 'hogging'. At sea this problem is compounded by the action of waves that not only induce roll which causes racking (shearing deformation) of the transverse shape of the hull, but also impose ceaselessly-changing buoyancy variations along the hull's length, leading to imbalances between weight and buoyancy which induce further stress. The varying stresses induced longitudinally in a wooden hull, generate shearing stresses that tend to make one part of the hull slide past the next. Induced stress-reversals within the hull weaken the fastenings and 'start' the planking of plank-first (edge-fastened) boats. Hence the emphasis in former times, on the use of strong plank fastenings, secured at both ends: clenched nails or treenails with a head at one end and a wedge at the other. In a frame-first (non edge-fastened) vessel these stresses can force out the caulking, thereby weakening the hull's watertight integrity.

Hull Shape and Size

The general hull shape has to match the function of the vessel and to minimise resistance to motion. The vessel's lines should allow the water displaced by the bow and entry of the vessel to move downwards and astern, and then to rise diagonally along the quarter (buttock lines) back to the surface, leaving the vessel with minimum turbulence at the stern. The requirement for speed and manoeuvrability should be considered when determining the relationship between length (L) and breadth (B). Capacity and stability should similarly be considered in conjunction with the relationship between (B) and depth (D).

Length and breadth
A longer boat (other conditions remaining equal) has the potential to achieve a higher speed since the speed at which wave-making becomes significant is increased, although this effect has to be balanced against the increase in wetted area hence greater skin-friction. A beamier boat, on the other hand, has greater stability and should have greater cargo capacity. At the same displacement, a narrower boat will have less transverse stability but with a greater (L/B) ratio will be more directionally stable, thus more difficult to manoeuvre.

Depth of hull and draft
Depth of hull amidships will generally determine freeboard and draft at any one displacement. In a vessel with a watertight deck at the level of the top of the sides (or in an open boat in which water does not come over the sides), freeboard is a measure of reserve of buoyancy and determines the maximum angle to which a boat can be heeled and still have a righting moment.

Potential Performance
Performance assessments may be made by eye, by coefficients (e.g. L/B, B/D) or by calculations using hydrostatic curves. Size and hull shape give a boat buoyancy and stability and thus determine a boat's capabilities, but their action is constrained by the effectiveness of the propulsion outfit and by the seaman's ability to use this in the prevailing circumstances. For a warship, speed and manoeuvrability will be emphasised, whereas a cargo vessel requires payload and stability. Since some of these characteristics are linked, and cannot be simultaneously maximised, every vessel will, to a degree, be a compromise.

Speed
For speed achievable by a boat under sail to be increased, hull and rig must be matched, the propulsive force made greater, and aerodynamic

drag and hydrostatic resistance decreased. This latter component consists of skin friction, viscous pressure, (caused by such things as a blunt bow or a sharp turn at the bilge), appendage resistance, air resistance (drag), and wave-making (due to the interaction of two trains of surface waves, one from the bow and one from the stern). This latter component is the most significant element of resistance, and ultimately limits the theoretical speed which a boat of given waterline length can achieve.

Estimates of speed potential can be made using a number of coefficients among which are:

- Slenderness: L/B values greater than 5 indicate good speed potential
- Midships: A/BT values less than 0.85 indicate good speed potential
- Block: V/BLT values less than 0.65 indicate good speed potential

                                      Where A = midship area;
                                      V = underwater volume

Cargo Capacity

Cargo capacity depends on the internal dimensions of the vessel, the space occupied by crew and equipment and the reserve of buoyancy. This capacity may be increased by reducing the weight of the boat or the number of crew and by varying the vessel's transverse section. The actual payload that can be carried on a particular occasion will depend on the bulk density of the cargo and on displacement/draft/stability calculations. In medieval times, cargo capacity was related to the volume of cargo; nowadays capacity (deadweight) is related to the weight. Deadweight (W) is the difference between light displacement (weight of water displaced by the vessel and equipment) and loaded displacement (weight of water displaced by vessel, equipment and cargo). In order to make meaningful comparisons between vessels (ancient and modern) it is necessary to estimate the cargo capacity of hypothetical reconstructions using displacement curves to derive deadweight capacity, rather than using such functions as 'Builders' Old Measurement'.

In medieval times the problem of equating a weight with a volume, for costing and taxation purposes, was solved using a standard unit of cargo (a tun = a cask of wine). Medieval estimates of a ship's 'tuns burden' may best be turned into today's measures by these conversions:

- Weight: 1 tun = 2240lbs = 1 tonne = 1.6 botta = 0.5 last
- Volume: 1 tun = 60 cubic feet.

The phrase 'tuns burden' should be translated as 'the number of standard units (a wine cask of 2240 lbs, occupying sixty cubic feet) that a vessel could carry'. Subject to stability considerations, more cargo by weight could be carried of materials with bulk density greater than that of wine (e.g. metal ingots), and less of materials with lower bulk densities (e.g. bales of wool).

Cargo carrier or warship?
A wreck with a hold would have been a cargo vessel. Such a hold may be identified by its position amidships, transverse partitions and the absence of (upper) crossbeams. Other indications of cargo carrying are: rowing stations only at the ends of the vessel; dunnage present; relatively massive (possible closely-spaced) frames amidships; L/B less than 5; L/D less than 10.

Propulsion
Before the introduction of steam power, vessels could be propelled in four main ways:

- by water power: drifting by tidal stream or river current
- by muscle power: pole, paddle or oar
- by wind power: sail
- towing by man, animal or another boat.

Some forms of propulsion (e.g. by paddle) may be combined with steering. Moreover, two or more methods of propulsion may be used in the same boat: for example, sail with paddle, or pole with tow. Indeed, combined pole-paddles have been used in recent times in Estonia, and pole-oars – a forked wooden or iron foot being fastened to the end of the oar-blade – are also known in the southern Baltic. Working the tides (downstream with the ebb tide; upstream with the flood) leaves no artifactual evidence; use of pole or paddle generally leaves no evidence on the hull, but poling walkways were sometimes fitted to boats used on inland waters. Towing and propulsion by oar or by sail require special fittings on the vessel.

Drifting downstream or with the tidal flow
The main problem is control of direction. For a steering device to work a vessel has to be moving faster or slower than the water in which it is floating: thus propelling a drifting vessel would enable it to be steered. Alternatively, steerage-way can be achieved by slowing down a drifting vessel by, for example, towing a weight or small anchor.

Paddle
Paddles may be used by men standing, sitting or kneeling: the method used determines the length of shaft. Where there is a steersman in a paddled craft, he may have a larger-bladed paddle than the others. Most ancient European logboats appear to have been paddled by kneeling or sitting crew. Because of their relatively narrow, waterline breadth, European simple logboats have insufficient stability for sail, and some may even be insufficiently stable to be propelled by pole or by standing paddlers unless the crew keep adjusting their balance to compensate. Most European excavated logboats were also too narrow for oars to be used, unless outriggers were to be fitted, but, to-date, there is no evidence for this.

Paddles are seen in use on many Scandinavian rock carvings dated to the Bronze or Iron Age. Artifacts thought to be paddles have been excavated, some in association with a boat (e.g. the Hjortspring boat from Denmark). Some paddle-like artifacts may be digging implements, baker's peels or butter-making devices. Modern paddles have a variety of blade shapes: for example, some blades are near-aerofoil in plan and of a length equal to their shaft; others have shorter blades with a pointed end.

Pole

Boats may be propelled by a man standing at bow or stern pushing a pole against the river or sea bed: this action is known as punting. When the man walks along one side of the boat, from forward to aft, as he pushes on a pole, it is known as quanting or setting. Pommeroeul boat 4, a Belgian river barge from of the first/second century AD, had such a poling walkway. Length of pole is related to size of boat and expected depth of water: a 3.5m pole is suitable for a small boat, 6m for a larger one; anything longer would be unwieldy. Such poles may also be used as sail spar, depth gauge or as a mooring post. Where sea or river bed are such that a pole might stick in them, poles are shod with a wooden or metal terminal of Y-shape, or open-rectangular shape, or merely a single prong. Remains of such pole shoes have been excavated from Iron Age and Roman contexts in Germany.

Oars

Oars are levers of a second order with a fulcrum (pivot) on some part of the boat, usually the sides. Large oars, each worked by two or more men are known as sweeps. The 'gearing' of an oar is the ratio of the length outboard of the pivot to the length inboard: this ratio is generally between 3 and 4, but for a racing eight it would be nearer 2.5. Rowing (the general term for working oars at sea) may be in one of three modes:

- Pulling: the oarsman, facing aft, pulls the handle towards himself on the power stroke.
Generally, such oarsmen sit on a bench.
- Pushing: the oarsman, facing forward, pushes on the handle on the power stroke.
Generally, such oarsmen stand to their task
- Sculling: the oarsman works an oar over the stern with alternate push and pull power strokes.

Exceptionally, other postures are known, such as when oarsmen move from a standing to a sitting position during each stroke – very tiring!

Oarsmen may use one or two oars for pulling or pushing, but only one in sculling. When using a single oar, rowers may be double-banked with two men at each station (sitting on the same thwart), or they may be at alternate stations. In larger boats, (galleys) there may be two or more men at each oar. At sea, the normal spacing between oarsmen in the sit/pull mode is 3ft (91cm), with 2ft 6in (72cm) being the minimum.

The dimensions of the human body affect the relationship between oar length, gearing, and angle to the horizontal. Furthermore these dimensions place limits on the range of values for the horizontal and vertical distances between thwarts, seat and pivot: that is, they affect the 'rowing geometry'. Cdr Eric McKee (has shown that, for the sit/pull style of rowing (Fig. 1.10), with a man of standard height (1.72m), oar angles varying between 17° and 25°. Using the after edge of the thwart as datum:

- Datum to pivot (horizontal) HDp ranges from 28 to 41cm
- Datum to pivot (vertical)   VHp ranges from 18 to 21cm
- Datum to heels (horizontal) HDh ranges from 27 to 64cm

Such data is used when attempting to reconstruct the propulsion methods of excavated vessels. It should be noticed, however, that, at sea, oar angles of up to 40° are known, and that 'sit-pull' is only one of several styles of rowing. Moreover, complex rowing styles are known: for example, when hands are crossed (twentieth century currach rowing); or oarsmen sit or stand to one side of the boat, using oars of unequal length. Other variables are: angles of sweep may vary from 80° to 48°; rowing rates can be up to thirty-five or (exceptionally) fifty strokes per minute.

Pivots provide a fulcrum about which the oar is powered. Moreover, they act as a restraint during the recovery stroke, oars may be left unattended, safely trailing from them, and they allow the oarsman to use a reverse stroke when manoeuvring. Several types are known:

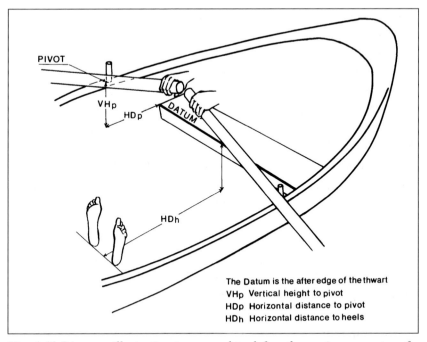

PIVOT

VHp

HDp

DATUM

HDh

The Datum is the after edge of the thwart
VHp Vertical height to pivot
HDp Horizontal distance to pivot
HDh Horizontal distance to heels

Fig. 1.10 Diagram illustrating terms used to define the rowing geometry of a boat. (after Eric McKee).

• Crutch: a U-shaped swivelling, metal crutch, proud of the top edge of the sides
• Oarlock or Rowlock: a U-shaped opening in the top strake or in a separate board.
• Oarport: round or rectangular holes cut through an upper strake.
• Two tholes: two wooden pins protruding vertically from the top strake.

Single thole and 'bull'
A hole in the loom of the oar, or in a 'bull' (wooden extension to the oar) fits over a pin protruding vertically upwards from the top strake. The oar is thus prevented from moving inboard, a major loss of efficiency. This type is used in several classes of seaboat, including the Irish *currach* and the Portuguese *xavega*.

Single thole and grommet

The loom of the oar is passed through a grommet that is fastened to the thole or through an adjacent hole. Hook-shaped tholes with leather grommets are referred to in Ancient Greek literature, but the precise method of use is not known. Maltese *dghaisa* harbour ferries, with thole and grommet, are generally propelled in the mode 'two oars/stand/push', occasionally 'one oar/sit/pull': oarsmen push or pull against the grommet. Whether this technique was used in the ancient Mediterranean world is not clear. In north-west European boats with this type of pivot, oars are worked against the wooden thole which is hooked to accommodate the oar shaft; the grommet assists oar control during recovery and acts as a pivot when oars are used to backwater.

Grommet

A grommet through a hole in, or near, the top strake is used in the mode one oar/sit/pull (India), and one oar/stand/push (Austria). A boat model from Ireland and a stone carving from the Rhineland, both of the first century BC, appear to have this simple pivot type.

Towing

Men may tow a boat by swimming and holding onto it, or when walking along a shallow river bed, but more generally it is done from the river or canal bank, when it is known as 'tracking'. In this latter mode, the pull is at an angle to the desired direction and will tend to move the boat towards the bank. It has been found empirically that, if the tow is fastened on the boat's centreline, at a station between 20% and 40% of the boat's waterline length from the bow, the boat will then be towed parallel to the near bank with minimum use of the steering device. To avoid obstructions on the bank, this tow may be fastened to a towing mast stepped at this point. Such tow lines were passed through a block (moveable up or down the mast), and on to a strong point aft.

On an excavated boat, a towing mast may be difficult to distinguish from a mast for sails. A square sail set on such a mast, stepped approximately 30% from the bow, with no balancing sail further aft, would restrict use to following winds. A lone, fore-and-aft sail, such as a sprit, lug or lateen, set so far forward could, however, be a more balanced rig. In general, for the same size of boat, towing mast steps are simpler and of less scantlings than sailing mast steps.

Sailing

American Indians used to harness the wind by holding up a leafy bush, a blanket or a piece of bark. Such 'sails' need no fittings on the boat and therefore cannot be detected archaeologically. When it is required to use sail in stronger winds and choppy seas, and to progress across or against the wind, permanent fittings are needed: a step for the heel of the mast, a mast-beam at top-of-the-sides level, and/or rigging (stays) running in the fore-and-aft direction from higher-up the mast to the hull structure (Fig. 1.11). Shrouds to the sides of the vessel may also be fitted.

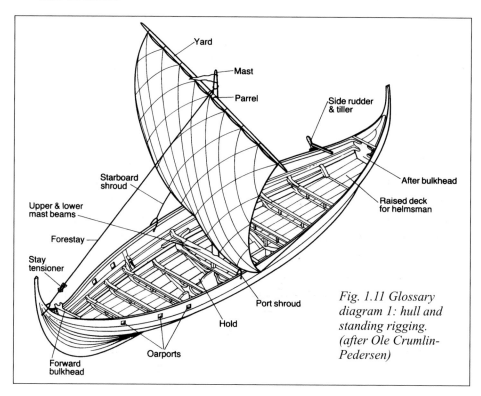

Fig. 1.11 Glossary diagram 1: hull and standing rigging. (after Ole Crumlin-Pedersen)

Labels: Yard, Mast, Parrel, Side rudder & tiller, Starboard shroud, After bulkhead, Upper & lower mast beams, Raised deck for helmsman, Forestay, Stay tensioner, Port shroud, Hold, Forward bulkhead, Oarports

Masted boats without such standing rigging are known, however, and even when there is rigging, in a small boat it may be of the simplest kind and made fast to thwarts or to timbers with a primary structural role. The excavated wreck of a sailing vessel may show little evidence of its former ability.

The minimum running rigging to ensure a well-set sail is a halyard to hoist and lower yard and sail, and ropes (sheets) to the lower corners to adjust the sail to the relative wind (Fig. 1.12). For windward sailing, braces to each yard arm would be needed, and a means of holding the leading edge (luff) of the sail firmly into wind would be advantageous (bowlines or beating spar). Lifts from the mast to each yard arm to support the yard and a parrel to hold that yard to the mast would be further refinements.

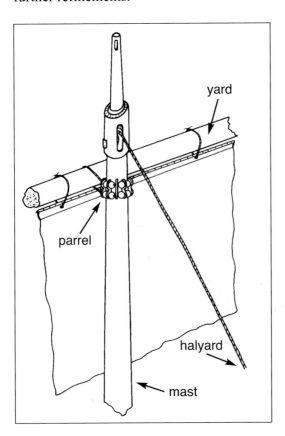

yard

parrel

halyard

mast

Fig. 1.12. Glossary diagram 2: running rigging. Note the halyard (used to hoist and send down the yard), and the parrel with trucks and ribs.

CONCEPTS AND TECHNIQUES

Square Sail (Figs. 1.11, 3.28)

This rectangular-shaped sail is bent to a yard set square ('at right angles') to the fore-and-aft line of the vessel, but which can be braced round some four to five points (45° – 56¼°) either side of the bow. Heeling and turning moments are imposed on the ship by the wind acting through the sail's centre of effort (CE) which is near its geometric centre. In response to changing weather, the vertical position of CE can be adjusted by reefing / un-reefing the sail, or using brails to increase / reduce its effective area. By late medieval times in north-west Europe, the position of CE could be further altered by setting or taking-in a topsail on the same mast. The turning moments engendered by CE are resisted by a hydrostatic force which acts at the hull's centre of lateral resistance (CLR), about which point the hull is considered to pivot around both the vertical, midships axis and the horizontal, fore-and-aft axis. This CLR is generally taken to be near the geometric centre of the underwater hull.

With a single square sail set on a mast amidships, CE and CLR will be separated longitudinally only slightly, thus inducing only a small, horizontal couple tending to turn the vessel into or out of wind. With CE slightly aft of CLR, the vessel will carry slight weather helm (tendency to turn into wind) – a desirable state. The couple resulting from vertical separation of CE and CLR causes the vessel to heel away from the wind until the new displacement stabilises the vessel in equilibrium.

It has been estimated that Viking Age ships with a single square sail would have made best progress to windward when six points (67½°) off the wind. To this must be added leeway (displacement downwind) of about one point (11¼°) giving a combined effect of seven points (78¾°) off the wind. Speed made good to windward would have been about two knots. Windward performance is important since it not only effects the time taken to make a particular passage, but also enhances the abilities of a ship in inshore waters to leave or make a landing place, or to round a headland. The analogy between a semi-rigid aerofoil such as an aircraft wing and the set of a flexible, variably-shaped sail is not a precise one, but the reason why an aircraft can fly is very similar to why a vessel can be sailed against the wind – not directly into the wind but at an angle to it.

Lateen sail (Fig. 1.13)

The lateen is a triangular sail bent to a long yard which is generally in the fore-and-aft line of the vessel. Such yards, which may be longer than the vessel, are generally made of two spars fished together at the centre, thereby allowing the yardarms to whip more freely and easing the setting of the sail. The mast for a lateen is stepped forward of amidships, and is usually raked forward since there is no forestay in this rig as such a line would impede operation of the sail. The yard is suspended on the leeward (downwind) side of the mast with its forward end bowsed down so that the sail is set with a high peak.

Fig. 1.13. A triangular lateen sail.

In general, the lateen has a better aerodynamic performance than the single square sail and is therefore more weatherly. On the other hand, the lateen is more difficult to handle – Columbus had *Nina* re-rigged from lateen to square before his first trans-Atlantic voyage, 'to obtain more tranquillity and less danger'. These difficulties arise because, when changing tack, the long, lateen yard, in an almost vertical attitude, is swung around, and forward of, the mast so that it can be re-set to the new leeward side. Furthermore, when running with the wind from astern, there is a danger that CE may get well ahead of CLR causing, not only steering problems but also, in the worst case, the vessel may dig in her head and plunge!

The so-called 'Arab' lateen (a quadrilateral sail with a short luff – a settee), was used in the Mediterranean from at least the second century AD, and the 'pure', triangular lateen from the sixth (possibly, fourth) century. A sail similar in shape to the latter was used in pre-Columbian, South American waters.

Sprit sail (Fig. 1.14)

The sprit is a four-sided, loose-footed, fore-and-aft sail spread by a sprit (spar) from peak to tack where it is held to the mast in a rope snotter. The mast is stepped forward of amidships bringing CE slightly forward of CLR. This rig gives manoeuvrability and weatherly performance and, with a small sail, is relatively easy to set and to drop: a large sprit sail requires complex reefing. The sprit was used in the eastern Mediterranean from at least the second century BC, but is not documented in north-west European waters before the fifteenth century.

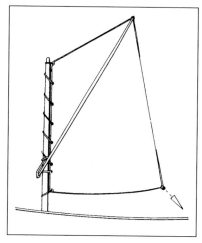

Fig. 1.14. A sprit sail. (after Eric McKee)

Lug sail (Fig. 3.22)

The lug is a four-sided, loose-footed, fore-and-aft sail set on a lug (yard) suspended from the mast so that ⅓ to ¼ of sail area is forward of the mast. When changing tack, the yard and sail are partly lowered (dipped) to allow the leading end of the lug and the tack of the sail to be passed abaft the mast to the new lee side. When only ¼ of the sail is forward, it is convenient to leave it to windward for short tacks and use it as a standing lug. To counteract movement aft of CE when the sail is reefed, the tack is bowsed well down thereby raking the sail. This sail draws well and works well to windward, but a strong, co-ordinated effort is necessary when 'dipping the lug'. A lugsail is probably depicted on two representations of Romano-Celtic boats of the second/third century AD.

Steering

A steering device is used to keep a vessel on a given heading relative to the wind or some other datum, and to alter that heading when necessary. Steering may be undertaken simultaneously, and by use of the same device, with certain forms of propulsion: for example, the poler or paddler may steer by using an asymmetric action as he faces forward to propel the boat. In the stand/push mode, oarsmen can also steer. For safety reasons, when oarsmen face astern, a helmsman is used or a forward-facing passenger may conn the oarsmen. On the other hand, when under sail, or when a vessel uses tidal flows or is being towed, independent steering is necessary.

All steering devices, to a greater or lesser degree, may be used to oppose leeway. Conversely, devices with the primary role of reducing leeway (e.g. guares – moveable leeboards) may be used to steer a craft as their attitude and position in the water is changed. Steering devices may be grouped under four headings:

Paddle
Steering paddles are generally bigger than those used for propulsion: they have to be of such a length that the blade is immersed when the steersman is standing. Steering by paddle leaves no detectable fittings or wear-marks on the boat.

Guare (firrer)
A lengthy, sometimes hydro-dynamically-shaped, wooden blade with a handle at its upper end is positioned in the fore-and-aft line of the boat or log raft and constrained so that it can be moved only in the vertical plane, but can be re-positioned elsewhere. As the immersed area of this blade is varied, by lowering or raising the guares, its turning effect on the vessel is varied. In South American waters, seventeenth century Europeans noted seagoing, sailing log rafts being steered and manoeuvred by varying the position and the depth of immersion of several of these devices. They were also used in sailing, log or bamboo rafts in Chinese, South-east Asian and Indian waters.

Steering oar or sweep
A large, specially-shaped oar pivoted at the stern, on the quarter, at the stem or on the bow. Larger ones (sweeps) are prevented from rotating by being wedged between two tholes or are pivoted on a single thole; they are operated by positioning the blade in the direction it is desired

to go – thus they work principally by increasing drag on that side of the vessel. Smaller ones, on the other hand, are worked within a crutch or rowlock and therefore may be rotated as well as displaced to one side; they thus gain turning force by varying the angle of attack.

In vessels with a wide range of draft and freeboard (such as river barges), the steering oar has to be used from two different levels corresponding to deep and light draft: there can be two related wear marks on the oar's loom, as seen on a 10m. steering oar recovered from Lake Neuchatel at Bevaix in Switzerland. Steering oars, dated to Roman times, with mortices in line with the blade and thus usable with an overhead tiller, have been excavated from Lake Nemi, Italy: this steering action is depicted on the first century AD monument to Blussus (now in Mainz Museum).

Rudder

A rudder has a shaped blade of (near) aerofoil section with a stock above it, to which is attached a tiller. It is mounted either at the stern (a median rudder) where, in neutral position, the tiller lies fore-and-aft, or on the quarter (side rudder – Figs. 1.11, 3.30) when the neutral tiller lies athwartships. Such rudders are fastened to the hull at two points which become the near-vertical axis about which the rudder blade is rotated. Alternatively, the rudder stock may be housed in a sleeve. Several medieval side rudders have been excavated, some loose and some with their parent vessel. Median rudders are well represented on north-west European town seals of the thirteenth and fourteenth centuries.

Side rudders may be used singly or one each to port and starboard. In the latter case, when the boat heels, changes in the immersed blade area are minimised.

Effects of steering devices

In a similar manner to the effect of airflow over an aircraft wing or a sail, steering devices (especially those not hand-held) generate lift and drag when immersed at a suitable angle to relative water flow. In their neutral position, lift (in the horizontal plane) will oppose, and just equal, any turning moment induced by the relative positions of the vessel's CE and CLR. With a single side rudder or a guares, this lift should also balance the turning moment generated by the devices' position away from the boat's centre line.

When the helmsman moves the steering device (rudder or steering oar) either way (or vertically, for the guares) from its neutral position, a turning moment is applied to the vessel. Under sail, drift downwind (leeway) induces a relative water flow over a steering device: in the neutral position the horizontal lift thus generated opposes the leeway inducing it. When drifting with river current or tidal stream, a vessel has no motion relative to the water and thus steering devices are ineffectual. Steerage way may be induced by use of a combined steering-propulsion device or by slowing the vessel (using a sea anchor, a length of cable or a small anchor) so that the vessel acquires motion relative to the water flow. In the latter case, the steering device will act in a sense that is the reverse of normal.

Boats and ships are generally long and narrow, and the greater their L/B and L/T ratios, the more they are directionally stable, hence the greater force needed to turn them. They turn about their centre of flotation (centre of waterplane area); thus the nearer the steering device is to the stern, the less the force required to turn. Nevertheless, steering devices (especially paddles) are sometimes additionally used at bow as well as at the stern, but a helmsman near the stern is in a better position to appreciate changing situations than one at the bow.

DESIGN METHODS

It is now generally considered that, in the earliest days of building planked boats, when the plank-first building sequence was used, the boat's shape emerged as the builder added shaped plank to shaped plank, and fastened them together. The builder did not work from drawings or construction plans, but had the intended design 'in his head'. That is to say, he built 'by eye', using handed-on knowledge and his own experience to get the shape of boat that he wanted.

With the change from 'plank first' to the 'framing-first' sequence, when the boat's shape is determined by framing, it may have been

36

possible to build and erect that framing 'by eye', nevertheless, since framing held the key to shape, it would be a small step to retain framing elements from a dismantled boat and use them as a pattern to fashion the framing for another, similarly-shaped boat. In this way, the idea of 'designing' a framework may have emerged.

Worldwide, the earliest plank boats known to be built 'framing first' are three seagoing vessels of the first to fourth century AD of the Romano-Celtic tradition. Planking was not fastened together in these vessels; rather, individual planks were fastened to the earlier-erected framing. Such boats are said to have been built 'stepwise, framing-first with some floating timbers'. There are indications that design aids were used to obtain the required hull shape: a measuring unit of c.55cm (possibly equivalent to two human feet); moreover, the ratio of maximum beam to length of plank-keel to length overall appears to have been approximately 1:2:3. This suggests that a way may have been evolved of designing each framing timber using the builder's eye and 'rules of thumb'.

THE RESEARCH SEQUENCE (Fig. 1.15)
As in other specialisations within Archaeology, a principal task of maritime archaeology is the search for patterns and other regularities

Fig. 1.15. Diagram to illustrate the stages in archaeological research.

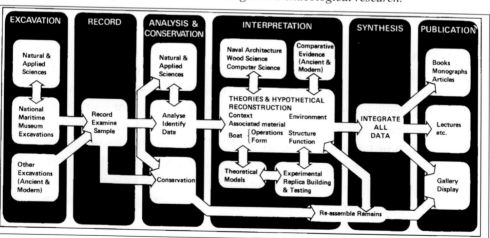

among the worldwide data amassed by excavation. Outside Europe, such evidence is rare and, even within Europe the earliest known form of water transport – a logboat – is dated as late as the eighth millennium BC. Excavated evidence is supplemented, by documentary and iconographic evidence when available, and interpretation is assisted by ethnographic data. Furthermore, all is illuminated, and interpretation further facilitated, by the sciences: material identifications, dating determinations, Wood Science, Physics, Naval Architecture and Environmental Studies (especially former sea levels). As Fig. 1.15 shows, the research path is a circular one.

Pre-excavation research and excavation

In theory, it should be possible to begin the sequence at the pre-excavation research phase where research by earlier archaeologists is evaluated, leading to field surveys in which places are identified where ancient vessels might have been deposited. To-date, however, very few sites of ancient vessels have been so identified: most of these being in burial mounds and in former lakes where local knowledge had survived. It might be thought that coastal waters would be a prolific source of wrecked vessels, and it is true that the charted position of many wrecks is now available and certain stretches of coastal water have a long-standing reputation as a 'hazard to shipping'. Before new land was gained in the Netherlands by the draining of the Zuider Zee, it was clear from documentary research that boats of all ages would be found there, and informative publications have resulted. Furthermore, one of the world's most important underwater sites, Skuldelev in Roskilde Fjord, Denmark, was first encountered by divers on reconnaissance: they recognised a medieval style of boatbuilding in the wrecks encountered. Nevertheless, several ancient craft excavated during recent times in north-west Europe, have been chance finds during development processes.

A significant number of early logboats and planked boats have been found during development of what are now land sites but were formerly in, or close to, lakes, rivers or the sea. Others have been encountered during the deep ploughing of land that had been cultivated for centuries; or, again, when the courses of rivers, especially their estuarine reaches, have been altered by natural forces. In these cases, pre-excavation research may not be possible and excavation may well be required to begin almost immediately.

During excavation, exposed timbers have to be kept waterlogged while they are exposed and recorded, until they are either lifted or re-buried. Timbers are examined as they lie, without undue disturbance; and samples are taken of the boat, its associated finds and the former environment, for laboratory investigation. If the remains are then to be back-filled, post-excavation analysis of the data recorded should lead to increased understanding of ancient boatbuilding. It is undoubtedly much more rewarding, however, to lift the boat remains – as a whole or in individual elements – maintain their waterlogged state and undertake further research in a laboratory environment. To the benefits of such controlled investigation of the recovered remains, may be added the advantage that, in the long term, it should be possible to put the conserved remains of the vessel on public display. Against these undoubted advantages must be balanced the costs of conservation and display.

Recording, analysis and conservation
After recovery, timbers have to be cleaned, individually identified and then immersed in tanks of water. If, like *Mary Rose*, the vessel is recovered as a coherent structure, a sprinkler system, rather than a tank, has to be used. Systematic recording of each timber by measured drawing and photograph is then undertaken, and wood samples examined for species identification and other scientific tests. Depending on the size of the vessel and other variables, a year would not be too long for this recording stage. The time taken to conserve, dry and clean the timbers for display must also be measured in years.

Examination of excavated wood
Detailed examination of excavated timbers can increase understanding of the ancient environment in which the parent tree grew, whether its growth had been managed, and what criteria had been used to select

particular trees. In north-west Europe, most excavated ship timbers are found to be oak (*Quercus sp.*); this is partly due to the survival characteristics of oak when compared with many other species, but is probably mainly due to the selection of oak for its widely acknowledged suitability for boatbuilding. Each timber's former orientation in its parent tree is identified, using the ring patterns and the fact that branch insertion is almost always at, or above, the horizontal. Knots (that part of a branch enclosed within the wood) disturb the normal, vertical run of the grain thus reducing timber strength. Many knots found in an excavated timber indicate non-optimal timber selection.

The general run of the grain (arrangement of the wood fibres) and the pattern of growth rings visible (for example, in the ends of a logboat) show how that log was converted from its parent tree: some logboats were fashioned from a whole bole, some from half of a log split vertically. The distinctive rays (layers of cells, in horizontal strands, running radially from the centre of an oak) that can be seen in a cross section of a radially-fashioned, oak plank may be used to determine the size the parent log, since the run of these partial radii can be projected to give the approximate position of the pith. It may then be assumed that the outer edge of each converted plank lies close to the heartwood / sapwood transition and thus the size of the parent log can be estimated. Where it has been looked for, sapwood has been found on at least some timbers (especially where a curve had to be worked) from almost every excavated vessel, showing that early builders strove to make maximum use of available timber.

Such examinations, supplemented by dendrological assessments, lead to a description of the parent trees of the excavated timbers. An example may be quoted from the publication of the Brigg 'raft':

'The five bottom planks of this boat were fashioned from three oaks: planks 1 & 5 from one tree; plank 2 from a second tree; and planks 3 & 4 from a third. The three forest oaks chosen were of straight grain. Two of them (trees 2 and 1/5) had few low branches, whereas, tree 3/4 had some substantial ones. The timber was narrow-ringed (0.67 to 2.57 mm), average ring widths being: tree 1/5: 1.54; tree 2: 1.50; tree 3/4: 1.20 mm. This probably reflects the crowding experienced from other trees. These three oak boles were more than 12.2m in length, with girths of 2.70 to 3.03m at breast height (1.5m); 2.21 to 2.49m at 5 to 6m.from the butt; and *c.*2.07m near their upper ends. It seems likely all three trees were damaged at their butt ends before conversion, with such damage extending further up the bole of tree 3/4 in the half that became plank 4.'

Interpretation

The data acquired during this examination, together with the excavation record, is then systematically investigated in the light of naval architectural principles, wood science, ship-and-boat building experience (ancient and modern), and ship-archaeological knowledge. The aim of this process is to build-up a picture of the vessel as excavated and of the environment in which she was deposited. The next stage is to build (plank by plank and frame by frame) an 'as-found' model of the excavated hull at, say, 1:10 scale. This is a model of the hull as excavated, but with displaced timbers re-instated, fragmented timbers restored, distorted, shrunken and compressed timbers rectified, and the hull rotated to its probable attitude when afloat. Computer programs may also be used for this task in a parallel evaluation.

After the 'as-found' model has been critically assessed and any necessary changes made, this model (or a scale drawing derived from it) can be used as the basis for attempts to reconstruct (hypothetically) the full, original form of the hull. If the overall length of the boat has survived (or extensions of the shape of the surviving parts of the hull can put a limit to it), and there is clear evidence for the height of part of the sheerline and/or the posts, an acceptable hull reconstruction is likely to be achieved; without such constraints, a valid reconstruction is unlikely.

Reconstruction of the propulsion outfit and the steering arrangements of a vessel can be more difficult than reconstruction of the hull, unless specific clues survive such as oar pivots, a mast step, rigging points, wear marks on timbers caused by rigging, or fittings from which a rudder could have been hung. Evidence from other excavated vessels of the same building tradition should provide useful comparators. It may be that a unique reconstruction proves impossible, and that, for example, two or more steering devices or sailing rigs have to be proposed as equally-likely solutions.

If a full reconstruction is achieved it becomes possible to make theoretical estimates of the original vessel's performance – stability, speeds achievable and cargo capacity, using coefficients and other naval architectural parameters. The reconstruction model, or a robust version of hull and rig, may be tank-tested in a naval architectural tank to get an idea of its prototype's performance in different sea states. Furthermore, a model under sail may be tested in a wind tunnel to gain further data on the vessel's performance.

River boat or sea-going?
The original prototype of an excavated vessel may be said to have been seagoing if it can be shown that, in the hands of a prudent mariner, and in normal, rather than abnormal, or even freakish, use it could be relied upon to carry a reasonable load on a sea passage of some duration in the weather and sea conditions prevailing in antiquity at that particular place. An unwelcome action in that reconstruction phase of research would be to embellish the 'as-found' model in a way that would suggest that the original vessel would have been capable of seagoing. Unbiased appraisal of the data arising from an excavation is essential.

The term 'seagoing' may be applied either to a coastal passage or to one in the 'open sea': these differ in the severity of weather and seas experienced, and in the availability of havens. Although stressful conditions can arise within estuaries and archipelagos, they are generally protected and have the advantage that, in the event of trouble, a vessel can put into a haven or take the ground on a foreshore; coastal passages in protected waters may be of a similar nature. Coastal passages with a long fetch upwind, however, can be as stressful as an open sea passage.

It is not possible to know the early mariner's attitude to risk, but we may assume that he was self-confident but not reckless in making use of his vessel's capabilities. It seems likely, therefore, that after propulsion by sail had been invented, prudent mariners would have undertaken passages within archipelagos and sheltered estuaries, rather than 'open sea' passages, until sail-use had been perfected.

The problem of deciding whether or not a particular excavated boat had formerly been used at sea may be tackled by considering the environment, the associated finds and the vessel itself. The environment investigated during an excavation is where the vessel was finally deposited and not necessarily where she had spent her operational life. River craft may be swept downstream to the sea; seagoing ships may be abandoned up-river as was the fifteenth century, *Grace Dieu* in the River Hamble at Bursledon. Furthermore, a vessel may have been deposited after being used in a role different from that of its working life – for example: as a river pontoon (the Brigg 'raft' in the Lincolnshire River Ancholme); as bank and sea wall reinforcements, (London excavations); or as underwater blockages (the Danish Skuldelev ships). Alternatively, vessels may be broken up and used as walkways or even 'fill' (Wood Quay, Dublin excavations).

As indicators of at least one overseas voyage the contents of an excavated vessel can be misleading. Exotic cargo, and even personal possessions, may be transferred from seagoing vessel to river craft for carriage up-stream. Ballast originating overseas may be embarked from a mound dumped by another vessel. Exotic species of hull timber may have been imported by some other craft. Barnacles or other salt-water creatures on an excavated hull should, on the other hand, indicate a seagoing passage, if only in the outer reaches of an estuary. The third way of determining seagoing abilities is by a critical assessment of the hull structure and the vessel's means of propulsion and steering. The accuracy of such assessments depends on the authenticity of the hypothetical reconstruction of the original form and structure that has been derived from the fragmented, distorted and dispersed, excavated vessel.

Even if such a reconstruction is judged, by this third method to be authentic, the assessment of the original vessel's seagoing potential is not easy since a number of interacting factors have to be considered: the strength, watertight integrity of the hull, its stability and its operational freeboard, manoeuvrability, controllability, seakindliness and dryness have all to be evaluated. An open boat below a certain size is likely to have been sea-going only in periods of relatively calm seas; on the other hand, a decked vessel (other things being equal) could have been regularly sea-going. A rockered bottom, a 'boat-shaped' underwater hull and a sheerline rising towards the ends suggest a seagoing vessel; a box-shaped vessel would have been restricted to river and lake. Since naval architects are very familiar with such principles, it is important that those of them who become involved in archaeological projects should be aware of the dangers of over re-constructing the 'as-found' version of the vessel, thereby giving the vessel an unwarranted seagoing ability.

A valid, theoretical reconstruction may also lead to the building and testing of a full-scale model ('floating hypothesis') of the original vessel. This is a different order of complexity when compared to the building and testing of a small-scale model. Moreover, whereas it might be possible to build a second, or even third, small-scale model to test different versions of hull or rig, this may not be financially possible at full-scale. Any full-scale model must therefore be thought of as a unique project. Providing archaeologists are rigorous in their attempts to reconstruct the full original form, structure, propulsion and steering, based on an authentic and rigorously-criticised, small-scale, 'as-found' model, theoretical assessments of performance based on that model are justifiable and are to be preferred to a necessarily-expensive, full-scale experiment. Proposals to build a full-scale reconstruction invoke immense publicity and seize public attention: in the event, several have proved to be more expensive, and to have contributed less to knowledge of the past, than anticipated.

Synthesis and Publication

The documentation of the research process, from 'Excavation' to 'Interpretation', forms the basis for the integration of the whole project so that publication may be by:

- Lectures and popular talks,
- Individual articles or monographs on technical aspects,
- A comprehensive volume on the project.

Until these targets are achieved, the archaeologist's duty to make his findings available will not have been fulfilled. Moreover, efforts should be made to press for public display of the conserved vessel.

Re-assessment
In the longer term, scholarly progress depends on there being published criticism of each project by experienced people. In this way not only does the sub-discipline benefit by the approval or the revision of such research, but also maritime archaeologists in general will be in a better position to undertake future projects.

THE EARLIEST WATER TRANSPORT
Worldwide, there is no direct evidence for any form of water transport until Mesolithic times, and it is not until the Bronze Age that boats other than logboats are known; a handful of European log rafts has been documented, but none before the second century AD. The earliest known representations of water transport are early-fifth millennium BC clay models – possibly of hide or reed-bundle boats – from Eridu in Iraq and Tel Mashnaqa in Syria; and a vessel with a bipod mast depicted on a painted ceramic, also of the fifth millennium BC, from Subiya in Kuwait. The earliest documentary reference to water transport is a Mesopotamian inscription about shipping, from the late third millennium BC.

Recent Arabian finds of fragments of solidified bitumen with reed impressions have been interpreted as the waterproofing outer layers of bundle boats. The earliest of these, excavated at Subiya, are dated to the sixth millennium BC. Such bundle boats have been used in recent centuries on the rivers of Iraq, near where natural bitumen is readily obtained. Boats similarly built were recently used by Chumash Indians in the coastal waters of southern California. The oldest-known logboats are from Pesse in the Netherlands and from Noyen-sur-Seine,

France: both are of pine, of a simple form without embellishments. The oldest-known planked vessels are from Egypt and are dated to the early third millennium BC.

These dates for water transport are simply not sufficiently early to match the evidence that human beings undertook seagoing voyages in very early times. For example, the first settlement of Greater Australia was before 40,000 BC, possible as early as 60,000. The Japanese islands were also probably first occupied around that time.

To attempt to identify the types of water transport that could have been used in those earliest days of seafaring, it is necessary to use a theoretical approach. With an understanding of the techniques used to build a range of boats and rafts in pre-industrial societies, and from personal observation, the materials, tools and techniques needed to build a simple and an advanced version of each one of the fourteen basic types of water transport can be specified. Secondly, we can identify the earliest technological stage (Palaeolithic, Neolithic etc) in which such tools and techniques are known to have been used. The earliest technological phase within which basic and complex versions of each type of float, raft or boat could have been built, may then be determined. These steps lead to the compilation of Table 1.1, a hypothetical assessment of the types of water transport that could have been built in four technological phases, and used in the Mediterranean and in north-west Europe (a zone of colder sea water).

That table indicates that the simplest form of planked boat could not have been built before the Neolithic and a complex version not until the Bronze Age. It is also notable that, in the Palaeolithic technological stage, only the three float types, simple rafts of logs or of hide-floats, and simple bark boats and hide boats could have been built. Of these types, floats, log rafts and hide-float rafts could have been used at sea in the Mediterranean, but not in waters further north than 40° N where low air and sea temperatures, combined with exposure to wind and wetness, would have induced hypothermia and thus taxed the crew beyond endurance.

TABLE 1.1. <u>Theoretical identification of early Water Transport.</u>

Technological stage	Water transport	Maritime environment	
		Mediterranean	Atlantic
Palaeolithic	Log float	Seagoing ?	Inland waters
	Hide float	Seagoing ?	Inland waters
	Bundle float	Seagoing ?	Inland waters
	Simple log raft	**Seagoing**	Inland waters
	Simple hide-float raft	**Seagoing**	Inland/no trad.
	Simple bark boat	Inland/no trad.	Inland/no trad.
	Simple hide boat	Inland waters	Inland waters
Mesolithic	Complex log raft	**Seagoing**	Inland waters
	Multiple hide-float raft	**Seagoing**	Inland/no trad.
	Bundle raft	**Seagoing**	Inland waters
	Simple logboat	Inland waters	Inland waters
	Multiple hide boat	**Seagoing**	**Seagoing**
	Basket boat	**Seagoing**	Seagoing/no trad.
Neolithic	Pot float	Seagoing ?	Inland/no trad.
	Pot-float raft	**Seagoing**	Inland/no trad.
	Pot boat	Seagoing ?	Inland/no trad.
	Stabilized logboat	**Seagoing**	**Seagoing**
	Paired logboats	**Seagoing**	**Seagoing**
	Extended logboat	**Seagoing**	**Seagoing**
	Simple plank boat	Inland waters	Inland waters
Bronze Age	Expanded logboat	**Seagoing**	**Seagoing**
	Bundle boat	**Seagoing**	Seagoing/no trad.
	Complex bark boat	Seagoing/ no trad.	Seagoing/ no trad.
	Complex plank boat	**Seagoing**	**Seagoing**

Using Table 1.1, we may say that, generally speaking, in the warmer waters of the world the first sea voyages – within sight of land – could have been undertaken using log or hide floats (possible ancillary to swimming), or simple rafts of logs or of hide floats. Outside these latitudes (i.e. north of 40° N and south of 40° S) the simple hide boat could have been used for short passages in the summer months. These early rafts and boats could have been propelled and steered by wooden paddles, and visual pilotage techniques would have been used. On present evidence, open-sea (out-of-sight-of-land) passages were first undertaken in the mid-second millennium BC, when propulsion by sail was widespread and advanced techniques were available to navigate without instruments. For such voyages, complex rafts, multiple hide boats, basket boats, complex logboats and planked boats could have been used, each in their appropriate region.

PILOTAGE AND NAVIGATION

Once a vessel moves so far out to sea that land can no longer be seen, a principal method of fixing position is gone: such a boat is surrounded on all sides by an apparently featureless sea within an unbroken horizon. Nevertheless, there are signs in the sea, in the air above the sea, and in the heavens, all of which can be used by the mariner to guide his vessel across this trackless sea to his intended destination.

The earliest sea voyages would have been in inshore waters, then coastal passages, with identifiable features on land always visible. During those times, voyages of exploration and settlement would have been undertaken in daylight, in fair weather and good visibility, with land always in sight either astern or ahead. On such voyages pilotage techniques were used: seamen became familiar with landmarks (the shape of a headland or the colour of a cliff, an isolated tree or a distinctive group of trees). With at least one of these in sight, the vessel's master would have a fair idea of his position. Seamarks (tidal rips, shoals, swash ways and sandbanks, and isolated rocks) would also have been noted, especially for guidance when entering and leaving a harbour. On such voyages the sounding pole or lead (earlier, a stone ?), were probably used in inshore waters – one is depicted being used from an Egyptian boat model dated to the third millennium BC. With such an aid the depth of water would be monitored thereby giving warning of approaching land and avoiding running aground.

The nature of the seabed could be ascertained from a sample recovered in the hollowed underside of the lead – another clue to the boat's position.

Most Mediterranean islands are visible from some point of land on the coasts of Europe: they were first settled in Neolithic times. Some of these – Malta, Cyprus and the Balearics – could probably not have been reached by paddled or oared boats during daylight hours, except during the days of longer daylight around midsummer. At other times of year, seamen may have left harbour before dawn; alternatively, it is possible that if, by dark, their destination could not be seen, they maintained their heading relative to Polaris (the Pole Star) or, with less accuracy, in relation to the wind or the swell.

By the mid-second millennium BC, when people from western Melanesia and south-east Asia began to settle the South Pacific islands, passages of several days' duration between widely-spaced islands meant that, for much of this time, land was not in sight. For such passages, advanced methods of navigation out-of-sight of land would have had to be used. It seems likely that these prehistoric seamen used dead-reckoning methods similar to those known to have been used by late-medieval Arabs, by nineteenth century Micronesians and, to a degree, by early-twentieth century North Sea trawler skippers. Courses were steered relative to a steady swell or wind, or, at night, to the Pole Star and its circumpolar constellation (Fig. 1.16). These headings could be cross-checked by noting the bearing of the sun at sunrise, sunset and at noon (sun at its highest). Speed could be estimated 'faster' or 'slower' in relation to known past performance. Alternatively, the passage of time, hence speed, could have been estimated by chanting a standard phrase, or by counting the number of oar strokes taken for the boat to pass a floating object thrown overboard from the bow. Accuracy in this form of navigation would have depended on inherited wisdom, on experience gained and on an eye for the weather.

Land still out-of-sight may be heralded by cloud sitting over it, by the flight-line of birds, by the boom of surf and by decreasing depths of water measured by sounding lead and line. Using distinctive

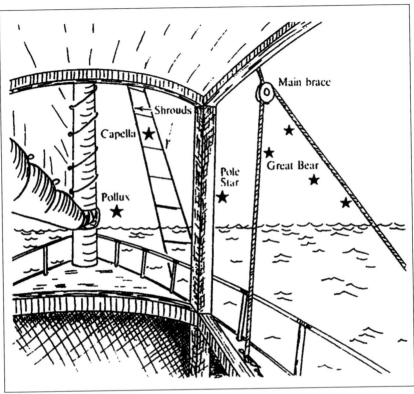

Fig. 1.16. Navigation without instruments: steering by Polaris & Ursa Major.

features – coastal outlines, and singular shapes of cliffs, headlands and peaks – the navigator would be able to identify his landfall when some distance offshore, and turn along the coast to his intended destination.

Apart from the sounding lead, instruments were not used to navigate at sea until the medieval period. The mariner's compass was first used, in Chinese waters, from the eleventh century; sea astrolabes and other latitude-determining instruments from the fourteenth century. The design of the latter devices may have been influenced by earlier Arab use of the *kamal* (Fig. 1.17), a simple instrument used to measure star altitudes that itself may have been developed from the *dioptre*, a Greek measuring device. By the fourteenth and fifteenth centuries, European ships had pilotage books (rutters), traverse tables

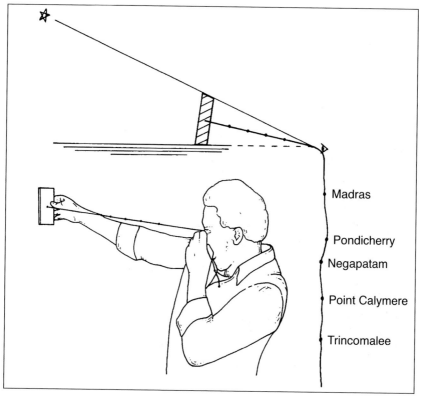

Fig. 1.17. A kamal, calibrated for the east coast of India, being used to determine 'latitude'.

(to convert courses steered into changes in latitude) and charts ('maps' of the sea). The difficult problem of determining longitude was not solved until the eighteenth century.

Landing places

From earliest times, and even today in many places, informal landing places were the norm: craft were used from the river bank or from the foreshore within a natural harbour, often where a stream entered the sea. Alternatively, ships were anchored in deeper water or made fast to a mooring post or stone. In the Mediterranean, where there was (and is) little tidal rise and fall, after vessels were fastened to a mooring post, they were manoeuvred until the stern touched the beach. In tidal waters, on the other hand, vessels 'took the ground' on a falling (ebb) tide and were subsequently re-floated by manpower or by the rising (flood) tide. On soft, muddy landing places, 'hards' were constructed of horizontally-laid hurdles, poles or withies so that boats would not stick to the mud. Causeways of similar construction were sometimes constructed across such foreshores, to and from dry land.

Formal harbours were first built in the eastern Mediterranean in the ninth, possibly eighth, century BC. They were intended to provide deeper water for larger vessels (ships), to alleviate the effects of silt brought down by the stream, and, on open sites, for protection from onshore winds and seas. When economics, politics, overseas trade or environmental changes determined, formal harbours were built elsewhere in the world. In north-west Europe, for example, during the tenth to eleventh centuries AD, demand increased for low density, mass-consumption goods leading to an increase in size of seagoing cargo ships. Having deeper draft, such vessels were best loaded and unloaded at deep water berths alongside wharfs. This requirement was reinforced by warehouse methods of marketing and the collection of custom dues. Formal harbours were therefore built and became focal points on overseas trade routes. Nevertheless, as may be seen on the late-eleventh century AD Bayeux Tapestry, informal landing places persisted elsewhere, and men and animals waded through shallow water to man, or to disembark from, their boats.

CHAPTER 2

The Mediterranean

The Mediterranean Sea is a semi-enclosed body of water, almost an inland sea, extending some 2,000 miles east and west and with a greatest breadth of around 700 miles. In longitude, it stretches from 6° W at the Strait of Gibraltar to 35° E on the Levant coast; in latitude, it extends from 31°–37° N on the coast of North Africa to *c*.46° N at the head of the Adriatic (Fig. 2.1). It is divided into two main basins by a seabed ridge that runs from Sicily to Cape Bon in Tunisia. The European Continental shelf, to the north, is generally narrow – out to forty miles in some places but only five in others. The seabed then drops relatively steeply to depths of more than 500 fathoms (900m).

Fig. 2.1. Map of the Mediterranean showing sites mentioned in the text.

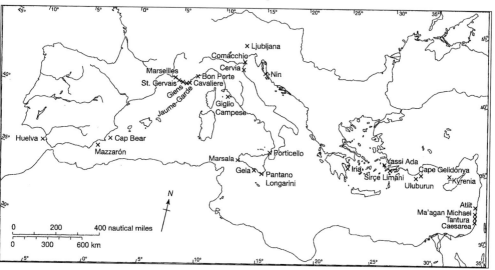

THE EARLY MARITIME ENVIRONMENT

During the Neolithic period, a time of lower sea levels, the islands and coastlines of the Mediterranean would have appeared very different from today. By 3,000 BC (in the Bronze Age), however, the Mediterranean sea level had risen to a height closer to today's mean sea level, and coastline and islands would have appeared generally as now. There have also been local, geomorphological changes within the coastal zone caused by tectonic movements, coastal erosion, silting, soil erosion, and the destructive and constructive works of Man. Nevertheless, seasonal winds, local winds, land and sea breezes and current flows of 1,000 BC are all thought to have been only marginally different from those of today. In general, therefore, we may conclude that, since 1,000 BC (Later Bronze Age / Iron Age), and possibly earlier, Mediterranean seafarers have faced environmental conditions similar to those we have today.

Tides and Streams

Generally, tidal range and tidal streams are influenced by sea level changes and coastline shifts, but the Mediterranean's virtually closed nature means that it is, and was, almost tideless. Only in the straits of Gibraltar, Messina (Italy/Sicily) and Euripus (Greece) are there now appreciable tidal flows, and only at the head of the Adriatic and of the Gulf of Gabes (Tunisia) are tidal ranges greater than one metre.

The generally cloud-free skies and high surface temperatures of the Mediterranean summer cause the rapid evaporation of surface water. The rivers that flow into the Mediterranean (principally, Nile, Po, Rhône and Ebro) replace only about one third of this water-loss, and equilibrium is attained by a strong, surface inflow from the Atlantic through the Strait of Gibraltar; simultaneously, there is a dense, highly saline, outflow at a lower level. Atlantic tidal flows, superimposed on this surface inflow, alternately reinforce and oppose it. The resulting flow is always easterly but varies from one to six knots. There are similar, but less pronounced, flows at the eastern end of the Mediterranean: water from the Danube, Don, Dneiper and Dneister, flowing into the Black Sea, more than compensates for evaporation. The resulting south-westerly, surface outflow from the Black Sea goes through the Bosporus and Dardanelles into the Aegean.

Close inshore, at both ends of the Mediterranean, there are contra-flows i.e. an outflow of water. At certain places on the coasts of the Gibraltar Strait such surface outflows are so strong that the inflowing, easterly stream nearly ceases and, indeed, on occasions, the flow sets westward.

Weather

For the past 5,000 years the climate of this region appears to have been much as it is nowadays. It is so distinctive that the term 'Mediterranean' is applied to similar areas in other parts of the world. Winters are short and mild, but can be dangerous with local, gale-force offshore winds and occasional, northerly winds bringing boisterous conditions and considerable seas, squalls, precipitation and thunderstorms. Moreover, there can be significant cloud-cover making night navigation by the stars difficult, if not impossible, and horizontal visibility can be much reduced, leading to pilotage problems in coastal waters. Summers, on the other hand, are lengthy, hot and with good visibility, long hours of daylight and little rain or cloud. The main seafaring problem in those months is that, on up to 20% of days, there is little or no wind. In general, within the eastern basin and in much of the west, the winds are predominantly from north and west. In the eastern basin, these 'Etesian' winds are highly predictable, and facilitate regular, summer passages from the Adriatic and the Aegean to the Levant and Egypt.

There was some winter sailing in the early Mediterranean, but it did not become a regular feature until the sixteenth century AD. In the late-seventh century BC the Greek poet Hesiod advised restricting seagoing to fifty days in July and August. The fourth century BC Roman author Vegetius gave a more credible picture: from mid-March to the end of May was risky; June to mid-September was safe; mid-September to mid-November was again risky; and from mid-November to mid-March the seas were said to be 'closed'. The six months between mid-April and mid-October (an 'extended summer'), appear to have been the regular, sailing season.

SAILING ROUTES

In the Aegean and the eastern Mediterranean summer, for a ship that could make-good a track at right angles to the wind (a not unreasonable assumption for the ships and sailing rigs of the Later Bronze Age), the regularity of the Etesian wind facilitated direct routes to the Levant and Egypt. This wind was so dominant that during the Aegean summer, there was little point in waiting for a wind that would be fair for direct, return passages to the Aegean. As an alternative, it would have been possible to sail an anti-clockwise, coastal route, using land breezes and other local phenomena that would, at times, overwhelm the Etesian wind. Failing this, the best time for a north-westward passage would have been earlier or later in the year, outside the Etesian season.

Beyond the Eastern Mediterranean, and before and after the summer months within that region, there was sufficient variability in wind direction, over a period of two to three weeks, for passages in several directions to be undertaken, providing that the master was prepared to anchor or remain in harbour, during foul winds. Generally speaking, delays encountered on such routes during late-spring and early-autumn were markedly shorter than in summer.

Passages Overseas

The east–west coastal route in the north

Mountain ranges and distinctive peaks within the coastal region give a recognisable profile to the northern coasts of the Mediterranean. They can be sighted from well out to sea – a distinct advantage. This coast, with its many natural harbours, has relatively deep water close inshore. Moreover, in the sailing season, with a predominant north-westerly wind, (apart from the northern coasts of Crete and Sicily) it is a windward shore. Furthermore, there are several large islands, from Cyprus in the east to the Balaeric islands in the west, which are visible from a boat before sight of the mainland is lost. Such islands not only acted as landmarks, but also provided shelter and fresh water when needed.

Passages eastwards generally had a fair wind in the open sea, but a slight, adverse current. Conversely, passages to the west had a favourable current, but generally foul winds, especially in the eastern basin. Summer voyages westwards would have been lengthy, using land breezes when available and remaining at anchor or in harbour, when not. Although, generally, this northern coast was not a lee shore, there were other hazards to overcome, especially near headlands. For example, at Cape Malea, the southern point of Greece, the westward-flowing current could be re-enforced by a north-east wind, making eastward passages impossible. Furthermore, the high ground to the north could deflect and intensify the wind, making even westward passages difficult. When attempting to sail around the Peloponnese, Jason is said to have been blown to Libya after encountering strong winds off this cape (Herodotus 4. 179).

On this northern route there are at least eight straits between the Bonifacio strait (between Sardinia and Corsica) and the Bosporus (between the Aegean and the Black Sea). Passage through such straits depended on the sea state and on the relative velocities of wind and current: in foul winds, ships waited in a near-by haven. Problems were not so severe in the wider straits, such as that at Otranto (between Italy and Albania), since funnelling effects were less. Moreover even in the narrower straits, such as the Dardanelles and the Bosporus, favourable, though weaker, counter-currents could be found inshore.

The east-west coastal route in the south

In summer, the Mediterranean southern coast was not only a lee shore, often with a heavy swell induced by the predominant north-west wind, but also was generally low-lying, especially in the eastern basin. Furthermore, in many inshore places there were reefs and shoals. Havens were rare, and there were very few islands – merely Pharos, west of the Nile; Kerkennah and Djerba in the Gulf of Sirte; and Malta, Gozo, Pantelleria and Lampedusa in the Sicilian channel.

Summer passages eastwards had a favourable current from

Gibraltar to the Nile, and a generally fair wind, though with an on-shore component. The passage through the Sicilian strait was difficult: a lee shore to the south, the wind funnelled by mountains, and shoals and reefs in the offing: the *Mediterranean Pilot* advises staying 'a good distance from the shore'. South and south-east of this strait lies the Gulf of Sirte with its low-lying coast, shoal water and drying, sand banks: vessels may easily be driven towards these hazards. Further east, the Nile delta was identified from seaward by its distinctive outflow and possibly by its relationship to the island of Pharos (where a lighthouse was eventually built).

A passage westward had the added disadvantages that it was against both the current and the wind: only west of Cape Bon was there a reasonable chance of easterlies. The passage northwards through the Sicilian strait was especially difficult, often impossible, as it was against the predominant wind, and the foul, tidal current could reach two to four knots.

Southern or northern route?
In addition to the advantages due to the relative maritime characteristics of these two routes, there are two other factors that favour the northern route:

The north coast was favourably endowed and relatively more developed, both agriculturally and commercially, than the African coast: vessels could, therefore, more readily undertake advantageous trading on the European coast.

Although there are coastal shallows and rocks along the northern route, it had the advantage that there was high ground within the adjacent coastal region, and many off-shore islands along the way. Thus a vessel could remain at safe distance from the coast, yet continue to have a known point of land in sight.

Routes across the Mediterranean
In addition to coastal routes at the ends of the Mediterranean, crossings could be made on open-sea passages in the central sector. One such passage was at the junction of the two basins: from Sicily, via islands,

to Tunisia. In good visibility, high ground, ahead or astern, is visible the whole time: Cape Bon (formerly Cape Hermes), the nearest point of land on the African coast, was a particularly notable landmark. Generally speaking, summer crossings of this seventy mile-wide Sicilian Channel could only be attempted by vessels able to make good a track at about right angles to the predominant north-west wind. In late-spring and in early-autumn, however, there was a better chance of having a wind from the stern sector. By the medieval period, this route was evidently in use throughout the year.

In good conditions, such passages would have been a 'long day's sail'. In poor visibility, however, it could have been necessary to delay approaching the African coast so that landfall would be made the following morning in daylight. Pantelleria was close to the direct route; the Maltese islands, Lampedusa and Kerkennah lay to leeward and could have provided a safety net when winds or leeway proved greater than expected.

Another possible crossing may have been from Crete to Libya, some 150-180 miles on a south-easterly heading, with the wind generally on the starboard side. This could have been one leg of a counter-clockwise voyage around the eastern Mediterranean: then from Libya to the Nile; next, using land breezes, northwards along the Levant, and westwards along the Turkish coasts; followed by a relatively-fast reach, across the wind, from Rhodes to Crete, albeit in a rough sea.

From the Turkish southern coast and the northern Levant, it would have been possible to sail direct to Libya, with the predominant wind on the starboard beam. An alternative passage was described by Odysseus: he told Eumaeus (*Odyssey*, 14: 300-5) that he had sailed from the Levant in a Phoenician ship bound for Libya. In a wind from the northern sector, they took 'the middle passage, clear of Crete'. This route would have been westerly, along the south coast of Asia Minor to Rhodes; then south of Crete; and from there, across the wind, to Libya.

Odysseus also noted that a passage from Crete to Egypt, a distance of some 300 nautical miles, took four days and nights, though some say three (Strabo 10.4.5). This would probably have been with the north-west wind fine on the starboard quarter. A return direct to Crete was impossible in the summer unless the vessel could tack well – even then it would have been a lengthy passage since the mean track would have been almost directly into the predominant wind. In late-spring, however, there would have been a 30% chance of a fair wind for a direct return. The alternative in summer would have been the counter-clockwise, coastal passage.

WATER TRANSPORT

Ancient boats and ships and small-scale models have been excavated in Mediterranean waters, and there are textual references to them and their uses. Much of the nautical information in Homer, Caesar, Strabo, Pliny and others is limited to generalised, and often inconsequential, observations, nevertheless, there are passages that alert us to special features of the maritime world or that, when combined with other facts, lead to deductions about ships, their builders, and the seafarers who sailed them.

Before the Bronze Age (up to *c.*3,800 BC)
Theory suggests that, during Mesolithic times, complex log rafts; buoyed rafts, bundle rafts, and complex hide boats could have been built and used in the Mediterranean. Although early examples of these four types have not been excavated, there is some literary and iconographic evidence for them, albeit of much later date.

Log rafts
In Chapter 1 Kings, 5-23 of the Bible, we read that, in the sixth century B.C, Hiram of Tyre had cedar and juniper logs towed by sea to Solomon. Log rafts were also used to transport elephants across the Saronic Gulf in 316 BC, and a log raft is depicted on a fourth century AD Contorniate coin.

Buoyed rafts
These were depicted on several sixth century BC Etruscan gems. Pliny

(*NH* 8.16) noted that, in the third century BC, elephants were transported between Calabria and Sicily on rafts buoyed by sealed pots.

Bundle rafts
It may be that bundle rafts, dated *c.*2,000 BC, are depicted on stones in the Maltese, megalithic temple at Hal Tarxien. Possible ones are also depicted on a Minoan gold ring of a similar date, from Mochlos in Crete. More certain is a depiction of Roman date, excavated at Bet She'arim in Israel, which has lines across the raft that probably represent bundle bindings. During recent centuries, reed bundle rafts were used off the island of Corfu to tend lobster pots: such examples of a 'living tradition' suggest a deep-rooted practice.

Hide boats
During Classical times, Lucan (Pharsalia, 4 131-2) refers to the use of hide boats in the Po valley. This appears to be the only reference to their use in Mediterranean countries, but they are known to have been used at an earlier date (BC/AD) in the Iberian Atlantic coastal lands in the west, and in Arabia to the east.

Early seagoing craft?
Of these four basic types of water transport, there is little Mediterranean evidence for the use of hide boats in ancient times or, indeed, today. For the log raft and the float raft there is evidence back to the late centuries BC: it seems possible that they were used in Mesolithic times. The evidence for the early use of bundle rafts depends on the interpretation of scribings and engravings. A more substantial point is that such rafts have been used in the Mediterranean during the recent past. Moreover, they were used in Egypt and in Mesopotamia at an early date. Suitable papyrus grows today in Sardinia, Corfu and Morocco, and it is known to have grown in Delos in earlier times.

This suggests that the bundle raft is most likely to have been the seafaring craft of the Mesolithic Mediterranean. Support for this

Fig. 2.2. A late-20th century experimental, reed bundle raft under way in the Aegean. (Harry Tzalas)

hypothesis comes from a recent experiment when a bundle raft, similar to those used off Corfu in the early-twentieth century, was built and used in the Aegean (Fig. 2.2).

By Neolithic times, in addition to those three types of raft and the hide boat, logboats of advanced design could have been built. Adding a stabilising log at the waterline to each side of a simple logboat, or pairing two logboats, side by side, would have had increased transverse stability and could have made the boat suitable for seagoing. Moreover, the addition of a washstrake to each side would have helped such a boat to cope with choppy seas. Logboats dated to the third millennium BC have been excavated from Italian lakes and rivers, and there are others that may prove to be earlier. Some of them may have been one of a pair, and one may have had its side extended upwards by the addition of washstrakes. These boats are too recent to throw direct light on the Neolithic, but they do prompt the question: if they had features making them suitable for seagoing in the Bronze Age, might they have been given similar features in the Neolithic?

Early Bronze Age – 3,800 to 2,000 BC

Depictions – models and engravings – provide information about the water transport of this period.

Models from Naxos

One of these, third millennium BC, lead models is in the Merseyside Museum, Liverpool; three others (one of which appears to be complete) are in the Ashmolean Museum, Oxford (Fig. 2.3). Their high L/B ratio of 12:1 suggests that the original boat was a logboat, possibly extended in height and length at bow and stern, with its sides built-up with planking.

Terracotta dishes from Syros

More than 200, third millennium BC, circular-shaped terracottas, with surrounding lip and projecting handle, have been excavated from Euboea, the Cycladic islands, the southern Greek mainland and, sparsely, from central Anatolia. Many of those from the Cycladic island of Syros have boats depicted on them. The lower end of these

Fig. 2.3. A 3rd Millennium BC lead boat model from Naxos, Greece. (Ashmolean Museum, Oxford)

vessels, rising at an angle of *c.*22°, probably represents the bow, since a high bow could have made the vessel directionally unstable. Other third millennium BC depictions of boats with one end higher than the other appear on two rock carvings from Naxos; an incised decoration on a vase from Orchomenos; and the stern of a boat on a pottery shard from Melos. The most likely interpretation is that, like the Syros engravings, they represent planked boats or extended logboats with high-sterns and crossbeams/thwarts, which were propelled by paddles.

<u>The Middle Bronze Age</u> (2,000 – 1,500 BC)
This period began with a marked increase in seafaring activity between Crete and the Levant coast. It appears to have ended around 1,600 – 1,500 BC with the collapse of the Crete-based Minoan civilisation that may well have followed a catastrophic volcanic explosion on the island of Thera/Santorini. Egyptian sources mention trading voyages to the Levant, undertaken by their ships, and a seagoing invasion. There is also textual, iconographic and artifactual evidence around 2000 BC for Cretan contact with the islands of Sicily and Cyprus, and with the west coast of Anatolia, the Levant and Egypt. Herodotus of 480-420 BC (1.171; 3.122), Thucydides of 460-400 BC and Strabo of BC/AD (10.4.8) testify to the seafaring reputation of Minos, the legendary ruler of Middle Bronze Age Crete. The earliest evidence for such Cretan vessels, and for the use of sail in the Mediterranean, are the double-ended ships with masts depicted on small, Cretan stone seals of *c.*2000 BC (Fig. 2.4).

Fig. 2.4. Sailing vessel on a Minoan seal of c.2000 BC: the earliest evidence for sail in the Mediterranean. (Ashmolean Museum, Oxford)

Thera frescos
In 1971, frescos with a maritime theme were uncovered on the inner walls of a house being excavated on the Cycladic island of Thera/Santorini. Dendrochronology and an Oxford Radiocarbon Laboratory assay indicated a Minoan date of 1628-1625 BC. Much

was missing from the ships depicted, and the elements that did survive were fragmented, but there appears to be no published record of these paintings as they emerged on excavation. It was not until after some restoration had been undertaken that the great majority, if not all, of the published photographs and drawings were made available.

Another difficulty in evaluating these frescos is that, although several attempts have been made to devise a system of reference uniquely identifying each one of the twenty vessels depicted, agreement has never been reached. At least four authors have attempted to reconstruct a typical Thera ship in the form of a lines plan, a scale drawing or scale model: these four reconstructions differ greatly from one another, not least in their overall dimensions. For example: lengths overall range from 17.6 m to 35m and breadths from 2.2m to 4.0m, resulting in L/B ratios varying from 6.49 to 15.45. It seems, therefore, that each re-constructor made different assumptions when attempting to fill the gaps in the surviving evidence. It will not be possible to attempt a valid reconstruction of the vessels that these Thera depictions represented until records of the frescos as first excavated are published – if such records exist.

The Late Bronze Age (1550 – 1100 BC)

Texts of the early fourteenth to the late twelfth century BC, excavated from the city of Ugarit on the northern stretch of the Levant coast, testify to trading voyages in a region that included Egypt, the Levant, Cyprus, the southern coast of Anatolia and the Aegean. Trade between Egypt and the Levant is confirmed by other documents excavated from El Amarna in Egypt, while light is shed on the Greek end of such voyages in texts found on clay tablets excavated from Knossos, Pylos, Mycenae and Thebes.

Wachsmann has drawn attention to numerous depictions (mostly broadside-on with the whole hull showing) of Mycenaean vessels dated to this period. These vessels are generally long in relation to their depth of hull and, longitudinally, they have a flat bottom that curves upwards at bow and stern, although the bow of occasional vessels is set at an angle rather than curved and some have a projecting forefoot. Many of these depictions show a deck raised above the hull on stanchions where fighting men are stationed. At bow and stern there are other decks: forward for the lookout; aft for the helmsman. These vessels were galleys, propelled by oars and by a sail set on a mast stepped near amidships and supported by stays. They were steered by a side rudder on the starboard quarter. Two underwater sites of this period, Cape Gelydonya and Uluburun, have been excavated off southwest Turkey.

Uluburun

This site was excavated by Professor George Bass between 1984 and 1994. The wrecked vessel had carried a wide range of goods including copper and tin. A two-metre length of the vessel was exposed. showing she had a plank-keel and cedar planking, some 60 mm thick and *c.*170-260 mm broad, which was fastened together by 20 mm thick, oak

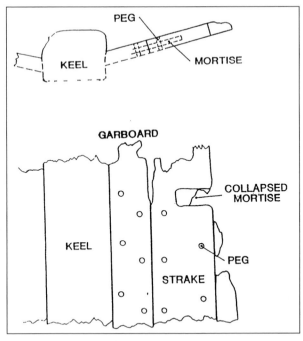

Fig. 2.5. Ulu Burun wreck remains. The circles on the plan represent treenails locking the tenons in position. (after Wachsmann)

mortise and tenon joints within plank thicknesses, and spaced at 60-240 mms intervals (Fig. 2.5). Unlike the known Egyptian vessels with this type of plank fastening, Uluburun tenons were locked within their mortises by trans-piercing treenails $c.22$ mm in diameter – the earliest known examples of this technique. No framing timbers were found and there were no signs of frame fastenings. This important vessel has been dated by dendrochronology to around 1305 BC: it seems likely that she was from the Levant.

Cape Gelydonya

In 1960, well before his work on the Uluburun ship, Bass investigated a site off Cape Gelydonya: further fieldwork was undertaken in 1987-9. The wreck, dated by radiocarbon to $c.1200$ BC, was probably that of a Levantine ship carrying a similar cargo to that in the Uluburun ship. As with Uluburun no evidence was found for the framing of this vessel. Although only a few fragments of the Cape Gelydonya ship's hull were revealed, they were sufficient to show that her planking had been fastened together by locked mortise and tenon joints similar to, but smaller than, those found in the Uluburun wreck. The limited extent of planking investigated leaves open the possibility that both these vessels had sewn plank fastenings, in addition to mortise and tenon joints.

The Early Iron Age ($c.1100$ to 550 BC)

Homer's ships

The *Iliad* and *Odyssey* epic poems were first written down around 750-700 BC: it is generally considered that they were based on earlier, oral traditions and reflect age-old practices. The *Odyssey* description of how early Greek ships were built of alder, poplar and fir, is both incomplete and enigmatic – probably because Homer was a poet, rather than a boatwright. It seems clear, however, that Homer describes a plank-first ('shell-first') building sequence. On the other hand, while some authors believe that Homer's vessel had locked mortise and tenon fastenings, others suggest that it was a sewn-plank vessel. A third, more likely, possibility is that Homer has described the building of a boat with both types of fastenings, as in earlier Egyptian ships and in boats of the eastern and central Mediterranean of the late centuries BC and the early centuries AD (see p.78–80). That explanation receives support from the fact that, in the *Iliad* (2: 135), Homer notes that the planking of the Greek ships investing Troy had rotted and their cords had worked loose.

In other sections of the *Odyssey* and the *Iliad* we read that masts were set-up in a mast-step and supported by a mast-beam, two forestays and a back-stay: when not in use, masts were lowered into a crutch at the stern. White linen sails were controlled by braces, brail/halyards and sheets made from leather, wood or papyrus. Pine oars were worked against a thole through a leather grommet. Ships were anchored off-shore in a sheltered cove using an anchor stone, and the stern was then brought to the beach in what later became known as a 'Mediterranean moor'. Occasionally they were propelled up the beach so that half the keel's length was aground. Otherwise, on suitable beaches, boats were dragged clear of the water, and held upright with props. Ahead of a storm, anchored ships would be beached stern-first and then dragged further inland. When a storm abated, beached vessels were unstuck using levers (a difficult task), and then 'run-down' into the sea.

In the late-fifth century BC, Herodotus (1:152, 163,166; 3:136; 4:148, 156; 6: 26, 95,101; 7: 25, 97,147) described three types of seagoing, sailing ship:

- thirty or fifty-oared galleys used on settlement voyages
- 'Broad-beamed' merchant ships. Possibly these had a few oars for manoeuvring.
- fifty-oared galleys used as fighting ships with a full complement of oars; some of these vessels had rams.

In those times, penteconters ('fifty-oared') were evidently the mainstay of Greek shipping, being used in almost every seagoing role. The term 'fifty-oared' may, by then, have been a measure of size, regardless of the number of oars or oarsmen.

Herodotus makes little comment on the performance of ships but in Book 6: 139-140, he seems to imply that Greek ships could tack on a fine reach, making good a track some seven points off the wind.

Depictions of ships
Vessels are depicted, in profile, on Greek pottery dated to the ninth and eighth centuries BC. Most of them appear to be warships, possibly penteconters, with a high curving stern and a ram at the bow. It seems likely that such vessels would be galleys, sailing with a fair wind and using oars in foul winds and when in action. On a few late-eighth century BC depictions, masts are indeed shown: by the seventh and sixth centuries, almost all have a mast, sometimes with a sail set. Moreover, the ram is shown being used offensively in a number of these illustrations.

Cargo ships and warships
From the eighth century BC, written sources distinguish between warships and cargo carriers. Specialised cargo ships were depicted in the Levant from c.700 BC and in the Aegean from the late sixth century. Warships, identified by a ram, are depicted from the ninth century, and warships of thirty and of fifty oars are mentioned by Homer. The earliest warship depictions are of monoremes; biremes (two levels of oars) predominate from the mid-eighth century. Phoenician biremes had a third, higher, deck on which armed men were stationed.

The Ram (Figs. 2.6 – 2.9)
Early representations of pointed rams (Fig. 2.9), intended to pierce an enemy hull at, or below, the waterline, are dated to the ninth/eighth century BC. Blunt-ended rams appear during the sixth century BC. Around 400 BC, 'trident' rams, with three broad, horizontal fins disposed one above the other, are depicted (Figs. 2.7, 2.8): these continued in use into the first century AD. Blunt-ended and trident rams were not designed to penetrate enemy planking but to thump the ship, thereby springing planks and starting the seams. The efficiency of rams, when attempting to break the oars of an enemy ship, remains to be investigated: it may well have been difficult in practice.

A trident-fitted, bronze ram recovered from the foreshore at Athlit (south of Haifa) and dated to the early-second century BC, is 2.26m long and would have enveloped the foremost two metres of its parent ship. After examination of wooden fragment extracted from inside this ram, Professor Richard Steffy concluded that the warship's hull planking had been fastened together before the ship's stem had been placed in position. The fore-stem was then fastened to the ramming timber by locked mortise and tenon and the two timbers together added to the hull. Subsequently, the ram was cast in bronze to match the shape of this bow structure.

The Trireme
Bireme warships, armed with a ram, seem to have been widely used in the eastern Mediterranean in the sixth and fifth centuries BC: they led to the trireme. Herodotus (1: 166) recorded that triremes were used in a Tyrrhenian Sea battle between Greeks and Carthaginians in c.600 BC, while, Thucydides (1:13) noted the belief that the first Greek triremes were built in Corinth. No wreck that could be interpreted as a trireme (or even a bireme) has so far been excavated. It has been argued that triremes were lightly-built and carried no ballast so that, if damaged in battle, they did not sink but were towed-away. On the other hand, it seems likely that a wrecked or stranded trireme would eventually become waterlogged when the remains would sink to the seabed. Moreover, Herodotus (6: 16; 8: 12) noted that triremes were sometimes run ashore and abandoned; furthermore, after the Battle of Salamis in 480 BC, captured Phoenician triremes were displayed at the Isthmus, at Sunium and at Salamis. Trireme remains may yet be excavated.

A Trireme reconstruction
In the absence of direct evidence, scholars, from the Renaissance onwards, have attempted to use documentary and iconographic evidence to establish the trireme's characteristic features. In the late twentieth century, much effort was put into a detailed evaluation of this evidence by Professor John Morrison, followed, in 1985, by the design of a reconstruction of a 'typical fifth century BC trireme', by

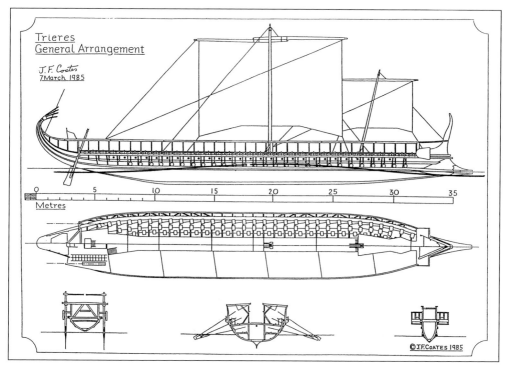

Fig. 2.6. Dr John Coates' plans for the hypothetically-reconstructed trireme Olympias.

naval architect, Dr John Coates (Fig. 2.6). During 1985-7, Dimitrios Tzakakos used these drawings to build a full-scale reconstruction at Piraeus: the vessel was subsequently commissioned into the Hellenic Navy as '*Olympias*'.

A fundamental problem encountered in the early stages of this project was the meaning to be given to the Greek term, *trieres* (trireme). Professor Morrison translated this as 'three-fitted' or 'three-rowing', and took this to mean that that there were three files of oarsmen on each side of the ship. Vitruvius (1.2.4) had given the distance between oarsmen as 'two cubits' and this distance was taken by the reconstructers to be the standard spacing in his day. Other documentary references indicated that some oars were slightly longer than others; that there was one man to each oar; and some oarsmen used outriggers. Further evidence indicated that the oarsmen within each group of three should be arranged at three levels, and excavated fifth century ship sheds, probably used by triremes, suggested the maximum lengths and breadths of such vessels.

Triremes were seldom, if ever, depicted under sail, since their main weapon was the ram used under oars. Owain Roberts, who reconstructed the rig, had, therefore, to base it on depictions of other ships' rig, supplemented by some documentary evidence that, for example, they had two sails, one larger than the other. Since no trireme has been excavated, hull structural evidence was taken from later wrecks such as the fourth century BC Kyrenia and the third century Marsala ships. Details derived from the remains of hull structure found within the excavated third century BC Athlit ram were also incorporated into *Olympias*' hull. The reconstructed trireme was built 'plank-first', with the planking fastened together by locked mortise and tenon joints; iron nails through treenails fastened frames to planking.

Trireme Performance

Under oars, high sprint speeds were achieved and three knots could be maintained for lengthy periods (Fig. 2.7). It was found, however, that dispensing with the lowest level of oarsmen made little difference to speeds achieved: these thalamians had insufficient space to pull a full stroke as they attempted to avoid crossbeams and other obstructions, and therefore contributed little to the propulsion of the ship. In good conditions, *Olympias*, rigged with square sails on main and foremast (Fig. 2.8), is estimated to have sailed with the wind one point or so forward of the beam (i.e. *c.*79° off the wind). If allowance is made for the observed leeway of one point (11¼°), it may be concluded that an ancient Mediterranean vessel, similar in hull and rig to *Olympias*, would have been able to make good a track across the wind and could have returned on the reciprocal track. During early sea trials in *Olympias* the two side rudders induced such a high drag that only one (and that, half-immersed) was subsequently used: any future reconstruction would have to incorporate less-bulky rudders.

*Fig. 2.7. Greek Trireme
reconstruction Olympias
under oars in 1987.*

*Fig. 2.8. Olympias under
sail in 1988.*

73

Assessment of the experiment

Other archaeological experiments have involved transforming the incomplete remains excavated, into a small-scale, reconstruction drawing or model from which a full-scale version was subsequently built, leading to the evaluation of performance underway. In contradistinction, the trireme project's aim was to design a reconstruction that would match documented aspects of performance while meeting constraints imposed by iconographic, historical and archaeological evidence. In the event, this aim proved to be unattainable, and, with hindsight, the Trireme Trust's interpretation of some of the documentary and illustrative evidence has been criticised, notably by Lucien Basch and by Alec Tilley. Nevertheless, a fair assessment of this project must be that both theoretical and practical aspects of the Trireme project have increased our understanding of early Mediterranean shipbuilding and seafaring. *Olympias* should be regarded as a 'floating hypothesis', the nearest we can get to the Athenian trireme of the fifth century BC, with the evidence available nowadays. The Trust has designed a revised version incorporating lessons learnt during those sea trials, including more room for oarsmen to ply their oars. The cost of building such a vessel would be enormous.

Phoenician seafaring

From the mid-second millennium BC to the sixth century BC a seafaring people inhabited the southern Levant coast. They were known to themselves as 'Canaanites'; in the Iliad they are referred to as 'Sidonians', after one of their principal ports. These 'Phoenicians', as they were known to the Greeks, were renowned shipbuilders, seamen and overseas traders who sailed out of Sidon and Tyre carrying Egyptian and Syrian goods around the Mediterranean. They were literate – indeed, they taught the Greeks to write – but little survives of their texts, and our knowledge of their seafaring activities is limited to Egyptian, Greek and Hebrew texts, and Assyrian and Egyptian depictions of their vessels.

For 1000 years, the Phoenicians were the principal traders within the length and breadth of the Mediterranean. They carried timber to the Israelites, timber, slaves and wine to the Egyptians, and a range of goods to Cyprus, Sicily, Sardinia Malta, Spain and the north African coast. From the mid-first millennium BC, they traded with Atlantic harbours beyond the Pillars of Hercules. In return, they gained raw materials such as gold, silver, copper and tin, all much in demand in the Levant and adjacent countries.

In the eighth century BC, a Phoenician colony was established at Carthage, in North Africa: colonies were subsequently founded in Malta and Sardinia and in Spain at Gadir (Cadiz). Peninsulas, or sites that, like Tyre and Sidon, were on islands, were preferred. At some of these natural harbours, artificial basins were built to increase capacity and to improve loading facilities. In the mid-first millennium BC Himilco sailed from Carthage along the Atlantic coast of Spain as far as Cape St Vincent, possibly even as far north as Coruña. Hanno similarly explored the African coast as far as Senegal in Cameroon, or possibly Cabon. Carthaginian coins have been excavated from the Canary Islands so it is likely that Phoenician seaman also visited there.

Egyptians, Persians and Israelites clearly recognised the seafaring capabilities of the Phoenicians. Pharaoh Necho II of the twenty-sixth dynasty (c.600 BC) despatched a Phoenician ship to attempt the circumnavigation of Africa, clockwise. Herodotus tells us that they took two-and-a-half years and, on return to Egypt, they reported that, as they sailed south and then west around southern Africa, the noon sun was to the north. Heredotus and his contemporaries did not believe them, but, to us, that statement is proof that they had sailed south of the equator and probably did achieve the circumnavigation.

The Persians, too, valued the Phoenician's seafaring abilities and included their ships in the Persian war fleet. Herodotus states that the naval power of Cambyses, son of Cyrus, depended on the Phoenicians, and they also were prominent in Xerxes' fleet at the battle of Salamis in 480 BC. Israelite scribes called the Phoenicians 'men who knew the sea' (1 Kings, 9: 26-8); another term was 'rulers of the sea' who 'did business with the nations in innumerable islands' (Ezekiel, 26: 16; 27: 1-3) 'whose traders were princes, whose merchants, the great ones of the world; whose goods travelled over the sea, over wide oceans' (Isaiah, 23: 1-8).

The Greeks, who from the eighth century BC began to rival the Phoenicians as explorers and traders, were not so sanguine. Nevertheless, from Homer to Strabo they praised the Phoenician's mastery of the sea. Strabo (1.1.6) states that they were the first in navigational abilities, a view that was later endorsed by Pliny (*NH* 7. 57) who noted that, after the Phoenicians had learnt astronomy from the Chaldeans, they became the first in the Mediterranean to apply that knowledge to the problem of open-sea navigation. They realized, for example, that the constellation Ursa Minor orbited the celestial pole in a smaller circle than did Ursa Major, and thus gave a more accurate direction of north. It is significant that this useful, but relatively difficult-to-identify, constellation became known in the Classical world as 'Phoinike'.

Phoenician/Canaanite ships (Fig. 2.9)
Mid-second millennium BC Egyptian documents mention cargo ships from the Levant coast. Although much is said in these, and other, documents about the cargo carried, little is said about the ships. The sixth century BC prophet Ezekiel (27: 3-10) described a Tyrean warship: she had a mast of cedar, oars of oak, linen sails and a purple and scarlet awning; the hull planking was fir or juniper, the deck planking, cedar or cypress. Vessels depicted on the early-fourteenth century BC tombs of Nebamun and Kenamun, at Thebes in Egypt, are thought to be Phoenician because of the distinctive dress of crew and merchants. The vertical sternpost of these ships is strikingly different from contemporary Egyptian ships which had a curvaceous finial at the stern.

By the ninth century BC, Assyrians had become overlords of the Levant states, and bronze reliefs on the Tell Balawat gates of Shalmaneser III show Phoenician boats bringing tribute to the Assyrian king. These craft have near-vertical ends surmounted by horse figureheads (*hippoi*). They are propelled by oarsmen standing to pull their oars, and are steered by an oar to starboard. A late-eighth century

Fig. 2.9. A Phoenician warship, with a pointed ram, of c. 700 BC on a relief from Kuyundjik. (The British Museum)

BC relief at Khorsabad, in the palace of Sargon II, has similar vessels but with vertical ends and a horse figurehead at the bow. These boats are towing timber baulks astern and are propelled by men who stand and push an oar. One boat, not towing timber, has a mast near amidships supported by forestay and backstay and there is a structure at the masthead – possibly a lookout position.

Another relief of 701 BC, from the Khorsabad palace of Sennacherib depicts the Phoenician evacuation of Tyre and Sidon by sea to Cyprus, as the Assyrian army advanced towards the coast. Cargo ships (with rounded hulls) and warships (under sail and with rams) have two levels of oars pulled by men standing and facing astern. Both types of vessel have steering oars. In the cargo vessels, on a third deck and seated beyond a bulwark, are women and men – some of the latter are armed. On two of the warships, armed men stand on a third deck; on the other three warships there are passengers and armed men. None of these ships has a figurehead: nevertheless, a horse-headed figure at the bow became a characteristic feature of Phoenician and Carthaginian ships. Strabo (2.3.4) noted that when Eudoxus, on his return to Egypt, reported that he had found a *hippos* off Somalia, he was told that such a figurehead could only have come from a Phoenician ship based in Gades (Cadiz).

Plank fastenings

Early Egyptian vessels, such as the *Cheops* ship (of *c.*2650 BC) and the Dahshur boats (of *c.*1850 BC) had unlocked, mortise and tenon plank fastenings in their hulls, nevertheless, the locked version of this joint was used in Egyptian artifacts found with these vessels. The earliest known locked, mortise and tenon fastenings in a ship's hull come from the Uluburun ship of *c.*1301 BC. Identifying the origins of an ancient shipwreck is always difficult, and a definitive answer can seldom be expected. Nevertheless, in the light of the cargo that these ships carried, Professor Bass, excavator of this and the Cape Gelydonya ships, considered that both were 'Canaanite, Syrian or Levantine' – in a word, 'Phoenician'. Moreover, it should be noted that the Romans called their mortise and tenon fastening, *coagmenta punicana* – 'Phoenician joints'.

Like clenched nails, locked mortise and tenon fastenings are positive on both sides of the seam and do not need to be reinforced by a second type of fastening. Nevertheless, as only a minor fraction of the hull of those two seagoing vessels has been examined, the possibility that sewn fastenings were used in their ends and elsewhere cannot be discounted. The balance of evidence suggests that both vessels were Phoenician seagoing ships: Phoenicians shipwrights had pioneered the use of locked, mortise and tenon joints to fasten together the underwater planking of seagoing hulls: such joints minimised water ingress and gave the hull more structural integrity in a seaway. This innovation must have further enhanced the Phoenicians' reputation for shipbuilding and seafaring excellence.

Sewn planking

Some of the early sewn-plank boats excavated in Britain (see p.109–120) and in south-east Asia had their planking lashed together by individual stitches. In contrast, other excavated sewn-plank boats, and all of those in use today, have their planking fastened together by continuous sewing. Moreover, most of today's sewn boatbuilders use treenail fastenings to position planking before sewing it together.

No excavated Mediterranean boat has had lashed planking, but several (dated to the sixth century BC) were fastened by continuous sewing: *Giglio* (off the west coast of Italy); *Bon Porté* (off the south coast of France); *Cala Sant Vicenç* (off Mallorca); and *Place Jules-Verne 9* (Marseilles). This sewing is along plank seams rather than transversely (as in the, earlier, Egyptian vessels). Sufficient of the Marseilles boat survived for her excavator to consider it probable that she was entirely sewn; the other boats may have been part-sewn.

There are several later boats (dated between 525 and 400 BC) with mainly locked, mortise and tenon plank fastenings that also have wedged, sewn fastenings in the lower hull, at the bow and stern, or in repairs: these include two vessels in Marseilles (*Place Jules-Verne 7* and *César 1*); *Gela 1* & *Gela 2* (off southern Sicily); *Grand Ribaud F* (off the south coast of France); and *Ma'agan Mikhael* (off the Israeli coast – Fig 2.10). Most of these vessels had caulking associated with their stitching, and the stitches in the *Ma'agan Mikhael* ship were wedged and sealed within their holes by resin. Before sewing, the planking of *Gela 1* and *Ribaud F* had been positioned by treenails within plank edges.

Parts of eleven sewn-plank boats, dated between the late-centuries BC and the eleventh century AD, have been excavated from lakes, rivers and deltas in the northern Adriatic, on both east and west coasts. Their flush-laid planking was fastened together by continuous sewing, but nails were additionally used in two of the boats from the Po delta. Treenails across plank edges were noted on the Ljubljana boat of *c.*200 BC, but not in other boats. The stitches of the Croatian Nin/Zaton boats of the early centuries AD, were wedged within their holes which were then blocked with resin and the outboard part of the stitches were cut away – a technique which ensured that stitches were not damaged when the boat took the ground or was dragged across a foreshore.

Today, worldwide, plank seams of sewn boats are caulked. In the early Mediterranean such caulking has been noted only on the *Gela* and *Jules-Verne 9* vessels: it may be that it was used in other excavated sewn boats but has not survived or has not been recognised. Sewn-plank boats are mentioned in the *Iliad* (2:135), the *Odyssey* (5: 244-57), and by several other authors from fifth century BC Aesychlus to the fifth century AD St Jerome in his *Epistolae*: in translation, those texts do not, however, distinguish between individual lashings and continuous sewing.

Excavated, Mediterranean sewn boats dated before the later sixth century BC appear to have had their planking positioned by treenails and to have been fastened with continuous sewing, each stitch being wedged within its hole. The majority, if not all, of these vessels are thought by their excavators to be of Greek origin. From the later sixth century, Greek builders of seagoing ships appear to have shifted to the use of mortise and tenon plank fastenings over most of the hull, with sewing restricted to the regions where leaks were most likely: the underwater hull, the ends, and in repairs. This shift from mainly sewing to mainly mortise and tenon fastenings may well have been the result of the sixth century Phoenician influence on the Greeks and other southern European people that has been recognised in other technological spheres and described as 'orientalisation'.

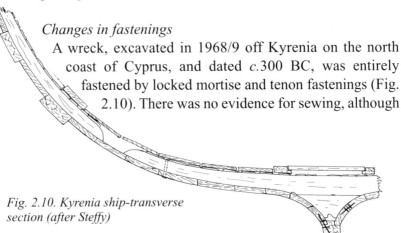

Changes in fastenings

A wreck, excavated in 1968/9 off Kyrenia on the north coast of Cyprus, and dated *c*.300 BC, was entirely fastened by locked mortise and tenon fastenings (Fig. 2.10). There was no evidence for sewing, although

Fig. 2.10. Kyrenia ship-transverse section (after Steffy)

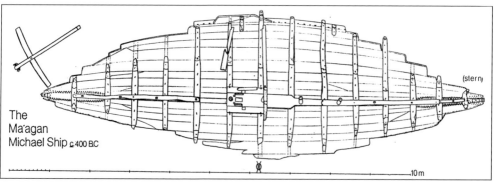

Fig. 2.11. Plan of the Ma'agan-Michael wreck. The zig-zag lines at bow and stern represent stitching. (Yak Kahanov)

sewing holes were found in one re-used ceiling plank. Nor were there treenails within the seams, and framing timbers were not lashed in position – rather copper nails had been driven from outboard, through planking and frame, and fastened by hooking each point back into the timber. Like *Gela 2* and the *Ma'agan Mikhael* ship (Fig. 2.11), this Kyrenian ship's hull had a 'wineglass-shaped' transverse section (Fig. 2.10). Her near-vertical, garboard (lowest) strakes enhanced the hull's leeway-resistance. Rabbets fashioned along the keel to take the garboard strakes were an innovation, as was the lead sheathing fastened to the planking.

On the limited evidence we now have, and with some assumptions, the main developments in Mediterranean ships' plank and frame fastenings appear to be:

Before c.2000 BC. Planking may have been lashed together using individual stitches. Subsequently, continuous sewing – sometimes with inter-plank treenails – replaced these conjectural lashings (as happened in north-west Europe in the early first millennium BC). Frames were lashed to the planking. This technological stage is comparable with the stage achieved (not contemporaneously) in Egypt, north-west Europe and south-east Asia. Unlocked mortise and tenons joints, together with sewing were also used in Egypt (and possibly elsewhere) to fasten hull planking together.

2000 to 1000 BC. Outside Egypt, the earliest Mediterranean vessels excavated are two second millennium wrecks from Turkish coastal waters: *Uluburun* of *c.*1,300 BC and *Cape Gelidonya* of *c.*1,200 BC. The former (certainly) and the latter (probably) had locked mortise and tenon plank fastenings. This fastening technique, which the Phoenician builders of these ships may have inherited from Egypt, subsequently spread to the central Mediterranean. In later times, sewing continued to be used in parts of the hull, and may well have been so used in the earliest Mediterranean ships with mortise and tenon fastenings – again, such a mixture of fastenings had earlier been used in Egypt. Frames continued to be lashed to the planking.

1000 to 300 BC. Vessels of the mid-first millennium BC, excavated from sites in southern Sicily, southern France and Israel, with locked mortise and tenon plank fastenings, also had sewn-plank fastenings in the lower hull, at bow and stern. Most of these boats had caulking with their stitching and, in some of them, stitches were wedged and sealed by resin within sewing holes. Frames were fastened to the planking by bronze or copper nails (iron was used in the *Jules Verne 7* vessel) clenched by hooking the point through 180°.

In the central and western Mediterranean, from the west coast of Italy to the island of Mallorca, sewn plank boats were built and frames continued to be lashed. In the Adriatic, plank boats with sewing along the plank seams (not transversely as in earlier Egyptian vessels) continued to be built into the early medieval period. A seventh century BC wreck excavated from Playa de la Isla, off south-east Spain, had locked mortise and tenon plank fastenings, with caulking in her seams; it is not yet clear whether she also had sewn-plank fastenings, but her frames were lashed to her planking.

300 BC –AD 500. A period of consolidation for plank fastenings, during which locked mortise and tenon fastenings generally, but not entirely, replaced sewn fastenings. In Roman times, this use of mortise and tenon plank fastenings spread outside the Mediterranean: westwards as far as Ireland (see p.123–4) and, as far eastwards as Vietnam.

Early centuries AD onwards. The long-established technique of fastening plank to plank to produce a watertight hull, began to be replaced by frame-first techniques: planking was fastened to already-erected framing. *Tantura A* boat (excavated from the Levant coast) was built in this sequence. Nevertheless, certain regions in the Mediterranean retained their former practices: sewn plank vessels, dated from the later centuries BC to the eleventh century AD, have been excavated from the Po delta, Adriatic lakes and rivers in Croatia and the west coast of Italy, and the island of Mallorca.

The Advantages of Change
From Sewing to Mortise and Tenon
The advantages of a change from sewn fastenings to locked mortise and tenon joints are that, unlike the unlocked version, locked joints are positive on both sides of the seam and may therefore be used as the sole type of fastening in a hull. Moreover, not only do the tenons act as discontinuous internal frames, reinforcing the hull transversely, but, when tightly-fitted, they also resist potentially-destructive shear forces which arise in any vessel afloat. As Dr Coates has pointed out, the particular boatbuilding skill needed before an entire hull could be fastened by mortise and tenon joints may well have been the ability to cut mortices at an angle within the thickness of a bevelled plank, especially where the hull shape, longitudinally and transversely, was changing rapidly. Until that skill was acquired, mortices and tenon joints were used only in the less-curved parts of the hull where mortices would be more-nearly aligned with plank faces and thus easier to cut. Sewn fastenings (and occasionally iron nails and treenails) continued to be used in the rest of the hull.

The earliest-known Mediterranean ship to be fastened solely by mortise and tenon joints is the Kyrenia ship of *c*.300 BC. By this date, such fastenings were so well-made that, unlike sewn-plank boats, no caulking was needed. Other improvements seen in the Kyrenia hull include sheathing the underwater hull with lead as an anti-fouling treatment and a barrier to teredo, and a framing pattern of alternating floors and half-frames.

From plank-first to frame-first

In a paper published in 2012, Patrice Pomey, Yaacov Kahanov and Eric Rieth re-assessed the evidence for the change from plank-first to frame-first that evidently took place in the Mediterranean during the fifth – sixth centuries AD. Using data from twenty-six excavated vessels, they established that ten wrecks (ranging in date from the late second century to the mid-fifth century AD) had been built in the plank-first sequence. During a transitional phase, mainly from the fifth to the ninth century, several other vessels built plank-first appeared to display signs of the change to frame-first. Such indications of a mixed approach are not so strong as to suggest that – like Chinese ships of the fifteenth century – Mediterranean ships built frame-first subsequently had their planking edge-fastened. Rather, the situation in the Mediterranean appears to have been one of experiment until frame-first techniques became dominant.

The earliest-known Mediterranean ship built frame-first is *Tantura A* dated *c.*AD 500. Other sixth to ninth century vessels from the Tantura site, and the *Serçe Limani* vessel of AD 1025, were also built in this sequence. In strict terminology such vessels, like those of the Romano-Celtic seagoing tradition (see p.124–134), were built in an alternating or stepwise manner known as framing-first (some framing then planking; further framing also followed by planking; and so on, upwards from keel to sheer). The full frame-first sequence, in which the entire hull is outlined by framing before planking is added, does not seem to have been used in Atlantic Europe until the seventeenth century AD; in the Mediterranean it may have been earlier.

The 'design' of early framing-first vessels

A change from the plank-first sequence to the framing-first sequence is also a change from building 'by eye', to building to a 'design'. In other words, before building begins, the builder needs the ability to mould ('specify' or 'design') the shape of key elements of the vessel to be built, possibly using battens. In mid-fifteenth century Venetian manuscripts on shipbuilding, the main hull dimensions are given as proportions of some modular unit, usually the keel length, the maximum beam or the length overall. The shape of the end-posts was probably deduced from a simple geometric construction using measured offsets, or by the use of a batten bent to the required shape through two control points. The shape of the master frame, a key feature of every vessel, was obtained using a 'rule' that defined the curve required at four points. The master frame, made from a master mould, was then made and set up on the keel near amidships. Similar frames were then set up on either side of this master, as far forward and aft as the constant, transverse section of the hull extended. The varying shapes of the remaining designed frames that determined the hull form beyond this central section, towards bow and stern, were obtained from the master frame by geometric means.

The main elements of this procedure are: design method; framing pattern and building sequence. The building sequence of most east-Mediterranean vessels built after AD 500 has been shown, above, to be framing-first; the general framing pattern of such vessels is also known. The third requirement, the specification of a design method, needs the definition of a unit of measurement (as Professor Steffy long ago pointed out in his publication of the *Serçe Liman* wreck) and the dimensions of the required hull to be specified (possibly as proportions of keel length or as multiples of the maximum beam). That measurement unit may also be used to define the shape of rudder, mast and yard.

Propulsion and Steering

Depictions of boats and ships with a single, square sail are known from 2000 BC (Fig. 2.4) until the Byzantine period. From the late sixth century AD, there are occasional depictions of a second square sail on a foremast or, from the first century AD, as an artemon at the bow. A third sail on a mizzen mast is mentioned in a mid-third century text and is depicted on a mosaic from Ostia. Fore-and-aft sails are depicted on small craft: a spritsail from the second century BC; a settee (a lateen with a short luff) from the second century AD; a lateen from the late fifth century AD. During the whole of this period, ships were generally steered by a rudder on each quarter.

Sails are exceptionally rare finds, but part of a second century BC linen sail, with an attached wooden brail ring, had been re-used as a shroud in the temple at Edfu, Egypt. Ezekiel of the late-sixth century BC noted that Phoenician ships had linen sails and Casson has noted that representations show that the edges of sails were re-enforced with bolt rope and the corners with leather patches.

NAVIGATION

Apart from the sounding lead, early Mediterranean seamen, like their counterparts worldwide, had no navigational instruments: instead they used methods based on inherited tradition, personal experience and informed observation of their environment. Homer's *Odyssey* includes descriptions of open sea voyages undertaken in this manner. Instead of a chart, Odysseus had a 'mental map' on which he 'plotted' his position relative to his home port or to his intended destination. When leaving Calypso's island (*Od.* 5.298-304.) he used the Great Bear (Ursa Major) to steer an easterly heading, and he monitored the rising and setting of Orion, Arcturus and the Pleiades: in other words, at night, Odysseus used a 'star compass'. By day, he used a 'wind compass' – eight elements of which are depicted on the first century BC Tower of the Winds in Athens. His standard unit distance at sea was a 'day's sail' (as in many cultures), and the passage of time at night was marked as selected stars reached their zenith. Odysseus also memorised landscapes so that, for example, when he sighted land after one lengthy passage he identified it as Pharos island, off the Nile delta; on another occasion, he recognised 'the wooded peak of windswept Neriton'.

On days of good visibility, each island in the Mediterranean can be seen from high ground somewhere on the European, African or Asian mainland, or from another island, or from a boat afloat when land sighted earlier is still in view (Fig. 2.12). Most of these islands had been colonised by the end of Neolithic times. Around midsummer, when there are up to sixteen hours of daylight, an oared boat in favourable conditions could be rowed in daylight to all islands (even the relatively remote Cyprus, Malta and the Balearics) from a near point on the mainland. On such exploratory passages, when land astern

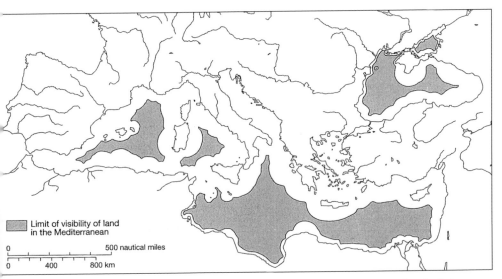

Fig. 2.12. Visibility of the Mediterranean coast from sea level. Ships in the shaded areas would be out-of-sight of land. (after Henkel)

or ahead is always in sight, the seaman uses pilotage methods, noting his position relative to his home port, or to his intended landing place, or relative to other recognizable landmarks that come into sight as the passage develops.

It is possible that, from necessity, simple navigational techniques were developed and used in poor weather, when land was not visible: for example, estimating directions from the Great Bear constellation at night ('north'), and from the sun's meridian passage ('noon') in daylight ('south'). Homer, Strabo and Pliny recognised the Phoenicians as 'master navigators': they were said to be the first to use astronomical knowledge, gained from the Chaldeans, to navigate at sea. Moreover, they were acknowledged to have been the first in the Mediterranean to recognise that the constellation Ursa Minor orbited the celestial North Pole in a tighter circle than did Ursa Major, and so could be used as a more precise indication of north. Lucan (*Bel. Civ.* 8: 177-181), of the first century AD, states that the zenith altitude of selected stars was measured against the mast (probably in harbour?)

giving some measure of latitude which could then be compared with similar estimates made elsewhere.

With the sky obscured, directions could be estimated relative to the wind or to the swell. In poor visibility, the sounding lead was used to detect decreasing depths of water, a warning of land ahead: Herodotus (2.5) notes that such was the practice when approaching the Nile delta from the north. Many such leads have been found in inshore waters, the earliest dateable one being from a wreck of 500 – 480 BC.

Such informal, environmental methods ('navigation without instruments') seem to have prevailed, until the sixth century AD when Arab seamen brought to the Mediterranean navigational ideas and techniques that they had developed from Greek land-surveying methods. In the ninth century AD the Arab navigator al-Khwarizmi described a staff which was used at sea to measure star altitudes: this 'prototype *kamal*' may have been developed from the Greek *dioptra*, a device for measuring angles. Thus the shift to mathematical navigation using instruments and charts continued, reaching its culmination in the thirteenth and fourteenth centuries.

In early times, pilotage and navigational lore was handed on orally, but in the fourth century BC, written sailing directions (*periploi*) for coastal passages began to be compiled. These were not only for passages within the Mediterranean, but also for selected passages outside. For example, along the coast of north-west Africa, and two routes southwards from the Egyptian Red Sea harbour of Myos Hormos: one around the Horn of Africa to Zanzibar, and another, beyond the Persian Gulf and on to India. This set of sailing directions, the *Periplus Maris Erythraei*, written in Greek in about AD 50, also included information on trading prospects and comments on the economic potential of coastal territories.

By the mid-first millennium BC, Phoenicians had sailed the Atlantic coast of north-west Africa, and traded along the Atlantic coast of south-west Iberia. In *c.*320 BC, Pytheas of Massilia (Marseille) undertook what was probably a scientific exploration of the European Atlantic coast, possibly going as far north as the Faroes and the Baltic. His account has not survived, but parts of it can be reconstructed from comments made by later writers. A *periplus* of the sixth century BC seems to have been incorporated by Avienus into his fourth century AD poem, *Ora Maritima*, in which he describes what was probably an established, southbound trade route from Ireland and Britain to Brittany; then along Europe's Atlantic coast to the Mediterranean, and eastwards between the Pillars of Hercules to Massilia; with a subsidiary route to Carthage. It is implied in this poem that the northern section of this route was undertaken by 'the hardy and industrious peoples of the islands and coasts around Ushant'; and the southern section – possibly beginning at Tartessus (near Cadiz) – by Mediterranean seafarers and merchants. In general terms, the southbound passage would have been more arduous and taken longer than northbound. That a lighthouse was built at Corunna in north-west Iberia in Roman times probably means that these relatively-difficult passages were still well-used in those days. In later-Roman times, north-bound trade (much of it in wine) appears to have gone via French and German rivers.

CHAPTER 3

Atlantic Europe

The 'Atlantic arc' of Europe consists of seas and coastal lands generally lying in a curve from Scandinavia through the western Baltic, Germany, the Low Countries, the British and Irish archipelago, northern and western France, Portugal and northern and western Spain. Much of this long coastline is open to the Atlantic Ocean. This maritime zone stretches from $c.63°$ to $36°$ N and from $11°$ W in the Atlantic to $c.20°$E in the Baltic (Fig. 3.1).

The Baltic and the North Sea are deposition regions with relatively shallow seas and low-lying coasts. Numerous tidal rivers flow into the North Sea, moving relatively slowly in their lower reaches through low-lying landscapes, their margins lined with reeds and marshes and with sandbanks where they enter the sea. In contradistinction, the coasts of Norway, France (as far south as the River Loire), Spain, Portugal and the western and south-western coasts of Ireland and Britain are formed of more resistant, solid rock, weathered into headlands, promontories and peninsulas, interspersed with bays and inlets. Generally, these are rugged coasts with bold cliffs and deep water relatively close inshore.

Along these coasts, from northern Norway, to the River Minho (at the Spain/Portugal northern border), with the exception of the south-east section of the Bay of Biscay, there are numerous off-lying islands. In certain parts, the coast is broken into a series of deep-water inlets such as fjords and rias, some of which have become natural harbours: in north-west Spain, Vigo and Corunna; in Brittany, Morlaix; in south-west England, Falmouth and Plymouth; in Wales, Milford Haven; in western Ireland, Killary; and in Norway, Trondheim, Bergen and

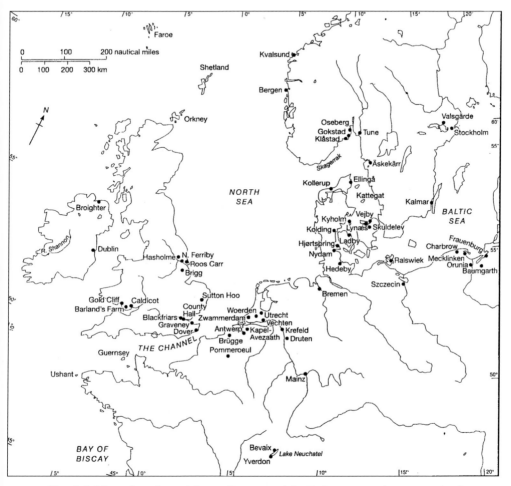

Fig. 3.1. Map of northern Atlantic Europe and the Baltic region showing sites of the principal boat finds.

Stavanger. There are also great tidal rivers, such as the Shannon in Ireland, the Severn and Clyde in Britain and the Guadalquivir, Tagus, Douro and Minho in the Iberian peninsula.

The Baltic is a tideless, relatively shallow, brackish sea with a mean depth of *c*.30 fathoms (55m). The Skagerrak, between Norway and Denmark, and the Kattegatt, between Denmark and Sweden, lead to three entrances to the Baltic: Øresund (between the Danish island of

91

Sjælland and south-west Sweden), and the Stora Bālt and the Lille Bālt (both of which pass through the Danish archipelago). These three entrances are only ten fathoms (*c.*18m) deep, forming a sill to the Baltic.

The North Sea is also relatively shallow, since it is part of the continental shelf, as is the Baltic. The seaward limit to this shelf has been recognised since medieval times to coincide approximately with the 100 fathom line (180m): a vessel to landward of this line is said to be 'in soundings'. Along the coasts of Norway and Iberia, and in places in the west and south-west of Ireland, the 100 fathom line is only ten to twenty nautical miles from land: entering soundings at these points becomes a warning of approaching land. On the other hand, the 100 fathom line is some hundreds of miles from the coasts of the Irish Sea, the North Sea, the Channel and the northern parts of the Bay of Biscay. On a passage from the Mediterranean to the Channel, a ship passes out of soundings when only *c.*20 nautical miles off north-west Spain, and enters them again when *c.*100 nautical miles south of Ushant. Other methods have then to be used to identify the entrance to the Channel to ensure that the ship keeps well clear of both Ushant and Scilly. In a similar situation, vessels from the south, bound for the south of Ireland or the Irish Sea, have to identify the channel between Scilly and Cape Clear in west Cork.

THE EARLY ENVIRONMENT
Past environmental changes in Atlantic Europe can, at present, be described only in the broadest terms, rather than the detailed descriptions that are needed to understand the maritime environment faced by earlier seamen. The best that can be done is to summarize, from the seaman's viewpoint, the present-day understanding of that environmental history during the past 12,000 years (omitting Scandinavia because of its radically different history during post-Ice Age times).

Before 3,000 BC
Before 10,000 BC Europe's Atlantic coastline would have been

significantly different from today. Between 10,000 and *c.*3,000 BC, that coastline would have increasingly converged towards todays.

From 3,000 BC onwards
Mean sea level has been within today's tidal range during this period: high water mark would have been above today's low water mark and slowly converging towards the high water mark we now have. The coastlines' general features would have increasingly resembled those of today and the tidal cycle and tidal streams would have been generally as they are today. There would, however, have been significant local differences in the appearance of the coast, since there would have been much less accumulation of silt in estuaries, and any spits and bars across estuary mouths would have been less prominent than they now are. On the other hand, coastal erosion, during the earlier years, would have been less.

Past climates are more difficult to deduce. It seems best, therefore, to assume – as in the Mediterranean – that from *c.*1,000 BC the weather, (including the predominant wind) has been not unlike today's, with many minor, and some unquantifiable major, fluctuations. Since there is little specific information about currents and tides until relatively recent times, twentieth century data on these important seafaring variables will be used when discussing the problems that early seamen faced.

The seafaring environment
Twentieth century data on currents, tides and wind may be assumed to apply to all periods back as far as 3,000 BC. Attempts to define such data for periods before that date are little better than guesswork.

Currents
The Gulf Stream leaves the Gulf of Mexico between Florida and Cuba, flows strongly northwards along the American east coast until, south of Nova Scotia, it is deflected eastwards by the south-flowing Labrador current. It then widens and slows to become the North Atlantic Current flowing in an east to north-east direction towards the Bay of Biscay

and the British and Irish archipelago. The southern part of this current is deflected to form the south-flowing Portugal and Canaries Current. The northern part splits into three elements: one through the Channel into the eastern North Sea; the weaker elements flow northwards to the west and the east of Ireland, then north of Shetland to the Norwegian coast.

In the approaches to the south of Ireland and the south-west of Britain, currents average ½ knot with a maximum of 1½ knots in strong westerly winds. There are south-flowing currents of up to ½ knot in the Bay of Biscay and up to one knot off the Iberian coats; eastward-flowing currents into the Mediterranean; northward-flowing currents on Ireland's west and east coasts; north-east currents along the Norwegian coast; weakish anti-clockwise circulation within the North Sea, and a parallel weak flow into the Baltic along the Danish coast and out of the Baltic along the Swedish and Norwegian coasts. These surface currents are generally slight – for example, only six nautical miles a day in the Channel.

Tides and tidal streams

Superimposed on those currents are the ebbs and flows of the tidal stream generated by astronomical forces, modified by weather and by local topography. Off the Atlantic coasts tides are semi-diurnal: two periods of high water and two of low water, each day. During each cycle, the tidal stream (a horizontal movement of the water) flows with increasing, then diminishing, strength in one direction for about six and a-quarter hours and then similarly in the opposite direction for another six and a-quarter hours.

The tidal wave runs northwards along the west coast of Iberia and then into the Bay of Biscay where it traces out an ellipse on a south-east/north-west alignment. From the western approaches to the archipelago this flood stream divides into three: east-north-east into the Channel and around to the Thames; north-east into the Irish Sea towards the Isle of Man; along the west coast of Ireland, through the North Channel towards the Isle of Man and around the north of Scotland across to Norway and southwards into the North Sea towards the Rhine and the Thames. Ancient seamen had to memorize those timings (in terms of the moon's phases) for all coastal waters they sailed. They also had to learn where contra-flows occurred inshore.

The corresponding vertical movement of the tidal sea is most apparent along the coast since the level moves from high to low water every 6¼ hours. As with tidal flows, these heights vary with the lunar cycle and with the weather, in particular the wind. The times of high water seldom coincide with the associated slack water (a forty minutes period without tidal flows) thus increasing the complexity of the data the mariner had to remember. Tidal ranges, the vertical height between high and low water, vary not only with the lunar cycle but also with local topography, being greatest at the heads of bays, gulfs and estuaries. Whereas the spring tidal range on an Atlantic coast is generally 1 – 2 fathoms, the range in the Bristol Channel and in the Baie du Mt St-Michel can reach 7 – 7.5 fathoms (13-14m). In the Baltic, as in the Mediterranean, there is little astronomically-generated tide and therefore negligible tidal flow. When winds prevail from one quarter for several days, however, and where there is a reasonable fetch, sea levels can alter by as much as 3ft (1m).

Winds
Throughout the year the predominant winds and the swell induced off Atlantic Europe (between Iberia and Denmark) are from the sector between south-west and north-west. In February to May, north-east and east winds are common in the North Sea region, and in the autumn, the north of the Bay of Biscay has easterly winds on a significant proportion of days. As in the Mediterranean, local features, such as headlands can modify the general wind pattern inshore, and in settled summer conditions there can be land and sea breezes, although not on the scale of the Mediterranean. From the north-west corner of Iberia southwards, predominant winds are from the northerly sector and there is more settled summer weather than further north. Summer winds off the Norwegian coast are generally northerly, backing north-west in the south. In the Skagerrak, west and south-west winds predominate in the summer; in the Kattegat and the Danish archipelago there are

variable winds with a preponderance of westerlies; within the Baltic, winds are from the sector north-east to south-west.

EARLY SEAFARING

The islands of Atlantic Europe were settled at an early date: Ireland was first settled before 7000 BC; Britain was re-settled after the Strait of Dover was created in *c.*6000 BC. The Hebridean and Danish archipelagos were settled during Mesolithic times; the Orkneys, north of Scotland, and Öland and Gotland, east of Sweden, in the Neolithic. These islands and island groups were all visible from continental Europe or from another island, and were sufficiently close that the longest passages would have been accomplished in a paddled craft, during daylight in settled summer conditions. Passages along the Continental coast would have been to the east, and therefore in the lee, of the chain of islands that lay along the Atlantic coast of Norway, Denmark, Germany and the Netherlands as far south as the Rhine estuary. There was a similar inshore route in the Bay of Biscay between Quimper in Brittany and the Gironde estuary.

The speed and range of these Mesolithic and Neolithic paddlers would have been limited. Raw materials, and traded goods such as stone axes and pottery, were transported long distances from their origin, but after a series of short sea passages. They would have made good use of tides and tidal flows that are a distinct feature of Atlantic Europe as far inland as the head of tide within estuaries, and would have acquired a detailed knowledge of the times of tidal ebb and flow, as well as of the sands and grounds in those estuaries and the swashways (relatively deepwater channels through otherwise shoal waters). Late-fifteenth century sailing directions for the '*Circumnavigation of England*' contain numerous references to tidal streams (and their timing in relation to the moon's phases), the tidal cycle and depths of water to be expected. They also noted sands and other shoal waters, prominent headlands and the like, and the directions such landmarks lay from one another.

Today in this region, gales of force seven and above are eight times more frequent in winter than in summer. Moreover, rough seas may be expected every fourth day in winter compared with every twelfth in summer; temperatures are significantly lower in winter, rain falls more often and lasts longer, and cloud cover is greater. It is likely, therefore that, in early Atlantic Europe, there would have been a summer seafaring season: during the winter months, coastal passages would have been avoided other than in exceptional circumstances, although fishing would probably have continued. As in the Mediterranean, late spring and early autumn, with their changeable weather patterns, would have included periods when seafaring was practicable. The seafaring season would therefore have primarily been May to September, with some passages also being undertaken in April and in October.

RAFTS, HIDE BOATS AND LOGBOATS

Since there is no excavated evidence for the types of float, raft or boat used in the earliest times, we must use the theoretical approach described in Chapter 1 (see p.45–48). Rafts can be used on almost all European rivers and lakes, but their use at sea is restricted to the zones of warmer water – say, between latitudes 40°N to 40°S. Thus – with the possible exception of the western and southern coastal waters of Iberia – it is unlikely that rafts were used at sea off Atlantic Europe.

On inland waters, during Palaeolithic times, several types of float, simple log rafts and simple hide boats could have been used for fishing, fowling and the gathering of reeds. From the seventh millennium, new lands were settled and, by this date, complex hide boats could have been used at sea, with complex log rafts, bundle rafts and simple logboats on inland waters. By 3000 BC the Shetland Islands, *c.*50 nautical miles north-north-east of Orkney, were settled, probably using hide boats and possibly complex logboats. There are no excavated rafts or boats to support such hypotheses. Although simple Mesolithic logboats, suitable for use on inland waters, have been excavated, the oldest – known European planked boats are dated no earlier than *c.*2000 BC.

It is convenient to discuss here those types of early water transport (other than planked boat) that are likely to have been used in early Atlantic Europe: rafts, hide boats and logboats.

EARLY SHIPS AND SEAFARING

Rafts

Of the two types of raft known to have been used recently in Atlantic Europe, log rafts have left slightly more evidence than bundle rafts. The latter type is scarcely mentioned, the earliest reference being in a late nineteenth century account of their use on Lough Erne in the north of Ireland. Raw materials for bundle rafts are, and were, widely available throughout Atlantic Europe. It is likely, but un-provable, that they were used on rivers and lakes from earliest times.

The only early log rafts excavated in north-west Europe are two of the second century AD recovered from the River Rhine near Strasbourg in 1938. Two centuries earlier, in the first century BC, Caesar (*DBG* 1.12, 6.5) had noted their use by Celts to cross rivers in Gaul.

Sarsens, the larger stones used to build Stonehenge, are thought to have been local, glacial erratics which could have been moved overland to the site; the smaller stones, bluestones, came from the Preseli Hills in Pembrokeshire, 150 miles to the west. In the mid-twentieth century, Professor Atkinson suggested that, log rafts had been used to ferry the bluestones from Milford Haven, along the south coast of Wales into the Severn estuary. From Portishead, near Bristol, they could then have been taken to Stonehenge on the rivers Frome, Wylie and Avon, with overland portages between them.

An early-third millennium BC coastal passage between Milford and Portishead would have been through seas with natural hazards – races, sands, rocks and shoals – and the feasibility of such a route has been questioned. The difficulties of such a passage should not be underestimated, nevertheless, the ancestors of those early-Bronze Age seamen had settled throughout the British and Irish archipelago and there is every reason to believe that their descendants, the seamen charged with moving those bluestones, would have coped with these hazards which, to them, would have been 'everyday' events. They would certainly have understood how to use tidal flows to advantage: indeed, it seems likely that the tides would have been their prime mover, paddles being used mainly to steer and to avoid hazards. Moreover, it is possible that they devised a way of using the rise and fall of the tide to solve the problem of loading and unloading the stones.

Hide boats

Caesar (*DBG*, 1. 54) and other classical authors, and medieval observers, mention the use of hide boats in the seas and on the rivers of north-west Europe. Moreover such boats are known to have been used in Wales, Scotland and Ireland from at least the seventeenth century, and they continue to be used in the west of Wales and of Ireland today (Fig. 3.2). A golden model boat (Fig. 3.3) of the first century BC confirms that this tradition goes back, at least, to Roman times. This small model of a seagoing, hide boat was found in the late nineteenth century on the margins of Lough Foyle at Broighter, near Limavady Junction in Co Derry, in the north-west of Ireland: it is now in the National Museum, Dublin. With it were eighteen oars pivoted

Fig. 3.2. The framework of a late-20th century curach nears completion in a County Kerry boat shed in south-west Ireland.

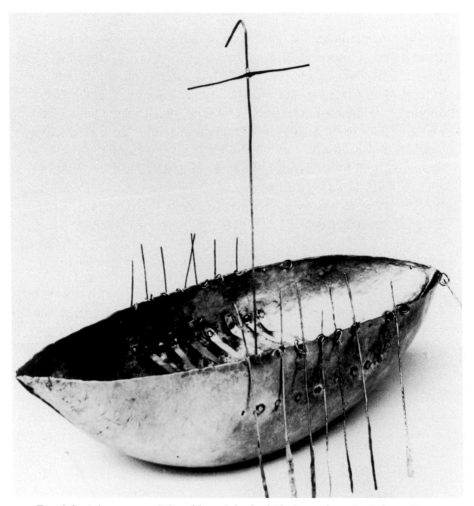

Fig. 3.3. A 1st century BC gold model of a hide boat, from Broighter, County Derry in the north of Ireland. (National Museum of Ireland)

in gold rings (representing rope grommets) near the sheerline, nine to each side, with each pair of oars associated with a rowing thwart. A mast and yard, stepped near amidships, suggest that a square sail would have been set. Poles for propulsion in shallow water, a steering oar for use on the boat's quarter, and a grapnel anchor were also carried.

100

Early hide boats?

Today, Greenland *umiaks* and Irish *currachs* do not have keels and their wooden framework is made of laths fastened together by lashings, treenails or iron nails. In contrast, the 'Wilde Irish' *currach* (Fig. 3.4) in a late seventeenth century drawing (now in the Pepys Library of Magdalene College, Cambridge) has prominent keel and stem, and an osier or woven-wicker framework: these distinctive features had been noted earlier by early medieval authors such as Adamnan and by classical authors Caesar, Lucan, Pliny and Dio Cassus. Such keels, stems and framing would have meant that early hide boats were not only stronger yet more resilient and energy-absorbing than their present-day counterparts, but also that they would

Fig. 3.4. A 17th century drawing by Capt Phillips of a 'Wild Irish portable vessel of wicker'. (Magdelene College, Cambridge)

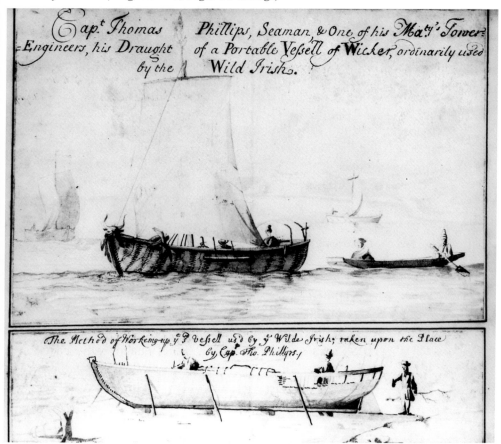

probably have been able to sail somewhat closer to the wind than their twenty-first century descendants. If, as seems likely, north-west European Bronze Age hide boats were similarly built they would also have had those qualities.

In theory, seagoing hide boats could have been built as early as Mesolithic times. They would have fitted well into that crofter-style economy, being quickly built (and repaired) from readily-available materials. Moreover they are used from informal landing places and are excellent through surf. Their relatively light weight means not only that they can be man-handled with ease, but also, being half the weight of an equivalent planked boat, have a good freeboard when loaded. Comparing like with like, hide boats are more seaworthy and sea-kindly than plank boats. Nevertheless, hide boats could never have been developed into ships: the hide contributes little, if anything, to the structural strength of the vessel, thus such boats are limited in length – the largest one ever recorded (an *umiak*) was *c.*18m in length.

Logboats

Logboats have been excavated from all European Atlantic countries, from Norway to Iberia. Simple logboats are made by hollowing a single log and shaping the ends and the outsides. They are thus similar in form to coffins, troughs, mill chutes, slipes and the like, excavated specimens of which can be mis-identified as logboats. Unless such boats have been fashioned from a very large log (as found, for example, on the west coast of North America) they do not have sufficient transverse stability to be used at sea. Such boats can, however, be turned into complex logboats by pairing, by expansion (after heat treatment) or by the addition of stabilisers, all of which increase the boat's waterline breadth and thus improve its stability. As the sides of a hollowed log are forced apart, in the process of expansion, the ends of the log rise and its midships height of sides is reduced. To restore that side height and regain the boat's level sheerline, a washstrake can be added to each side. There may, however, be other reasons for extending side height: the medieval English logboat, *Kentmere 1*, had been extended by five clinker-laid strakes after its sides had been reduced in height by decay or damage.

River boats or sea-going?

A logboat's transverse stability is determined by its breadth at the waterline: the greater that beam measurement, the greater the boat's stability. Generally, that waterline beam is itself limited by the diameter of the parent log. Moreover, the depth of hull and, hence, freeboard are also determined by that measurement. Logboats built from exceptionally large trees (for example, those on the western coast of North America) have sufficient stability and freeboard to be sea-going. Few, if any, European trees have been of that size and therefore logboats built there were not seagoing unless they had their stability increased by pairing, by expansion or by fitting stabilisers and had also had washstrakes fitted to increase their freeboard. Although washstrakes are thought to have been fitted to some western European logboats, there is no evidence, at present, that prehistoric logboats had their stability increased by one of those three methods. Until post-medieval times, logboats were used widely on the lakes and rivers of Atlantic Europe, and possibly within sheltered archipelagos. It is unlikely that they were ever used in the outer reaches of estuaries or at sea; hide boats and, subsequently, planked boats would have been the seagoing craft.

Mesolithic and Neolithic

The oldest known logboats are from Pesse in the Netherlands and from Noyen-sur-Seine, France: these were both of pine (*Pinus sylvestris*) and are dated *c.*7000 BC, relatively soon after the effects of the last Ice Age had ameliorated. Other Mesolithic logboats were of alder (*Alnus sp*), poplar (*Populus sp*) and lime (*Tilia sp*). Oak (*Quercus sp*) logboats appeared in the middle Neolithic and, by the Bronze Age, this seems to have become the preferred species. The earliest logboat finds lie in an arc from Denmark, through north-west Germany and the Low Countries to north-west France. Logboats were used in Ireland from *c.*4000 BC, and in Britain from the fourth millennium BC. In

Scandinavia (other than Denmark) they appear not to have been used until *c*.500 BC. They continued in use in parts of Atlantic Europe into the eighteenth century and beyond.

The Bronze and Iron Ages

Some Bronze Age oak logboats were more than 10m in length, with other dimensions commensurate. Furthermore, a range of woodworking techniques were used to build them: this point may be illustrated by reference to two boats from the River Humber region in eastern Britain. The Brigg logboat (14.78 x 1.37 x 1m) was found in 1886 when foundations for the Brigg Gas Works were dug near the River Ancholme, a Lincolnshire tributary of the Humber (Fig. 3.5). This boat was lost during a 1942 air raid when Hull Municipal Museum was destroyed. The Hasholme logboat (12.78 x 1.4 x 1.25m) was unearthed in 1984 during drainage works in a field (now below

Fig. 3.5. The Brigg logboat of c. 1000 BC after excavation from a former channel of the River Ancholme in 1886.

Fig. 3.6. The c.300 BC Hasholme logboat during excavation from a former tributary of the River Humber in 1984. The stern is nearest the camera.

sea level) near Holme-on-Spalding Moor, in east Yorkshire (Figs. 3.6 & 3.7). It is now undergoing conservation in Hull Museums.

These boats have a number of characteristics in common, some of them being due to the great size of their parent oaks each of which would have been 14 –15m in length of bole, with a lower girth of 5.5 – 6m. Such trees would have been 800 years or so old when felled, and would have weighed around thirty tonnes. Oaks of that age

105

Fig. 3.7. An 'exploded' drawing of the Hasholme logboat reconstructed.

invariably develop heart rot spreading up the bole from the butt end. In the Hasholme tree, but not in *Brigg*, the rot had spread to the top of the bole. This meant that, while *Brigg* had one open end (the butt end which became the stern of the boat), *Hasholme* had both ends open. To make these boats watertight, they each had to have their stern closed by inserting a transom board within a groove packed with moss; additionally, *Hasholme* had to have a two-piece bow incorporated to close her forward end. Both *Brigg* and *Hasholme* had *oculi* (representations of eyes) on port and starboard bows, and *Hasholme* also had two 'eyes' and a 'nose' worked on the after face of her transom stern. The primary function of the 'eyes' in *Hasholme*'s transom was to facilitate the lowering of that transom into its groove from above; the 'nose' was part of an arrangement that kept that transom within its groove.

The great size of the two parent logs resulted in them having other characteristics in common: for example, during the hollowing process, several beam-ties were fitted to hold the sides of these great boats together, until their open ends could be closed. There were also differences: the Brigg logboat did not have washstrakes and, also unlike *Hasholme*, it had ridges worked in the solid across the bottom of the forepart of the boat. Patches and other repairs to Brigg were sewn, wedged or fastened with treenails; *Hasholme* fittings and repairs were dovetailed in shape, or were held in place by treenails locked by a key (cotter). Such differences suggest that the Brigg boat was older than *Hasholme*, but possibly not as much as the 700 years suggested by published dates. A sample of wood from the Hasholme boat, including the heartwood/sapwood transition, was dated to *c.*300 BC by dendrochronology; a fragment from an un-recorded part of the Brigg log was dated by C14 to *c.*1000 BC.

With a five-man crew, at a draft of 0.60m and 0.40m freeboard, Brigg could have carried 5.5 tonnes of cargo; *Hasholme*, with a similar crew would have carried the same load at a draft of 0.75m and freeboard of 0.50m. Boats of this shape and size would not have been easy to handle within the Humber estuary, its tributary rivers and creeks. Logboats of less than half that length would have been handier and more readily manoeuvred. It may be that, in both cases, a near-unique tree was selected and fashioned into a logboat with the aim of enhancing the owners' standing. The size of both boats, the oculi in their bows, and the anthropomorphic look of the Hasholme boat when seen from astern, all suggest that both these logboats had been built to enhance their owners' special status.

Roman times and later
An increasing range of tools during the late Iron Age and the Roman period, led to advanced woodworking techniques in logboat building such as thwarts supported by knees and dwarf bulkheads dividing boats into functional spaces. Few boats now had fitted transoms, probably because the supply of large, venerable oaks had been exhausted and the younger oaks now chosen had sounder boles from which a watertight stern could be made.

Modifications to the simple logboat
<u>Expansion</u>. Crumlin-Pedersen has argued that some of the small oak logboats used as coffins in first to third centuries AD graves, on the island of Bornholm in the Baltic, had been expanded, that is, their sides had been forced apart and ribs inserted to hold that expanded shape. Such an increased waterline beam measurement would have given

107

them greater stability. Expansion has not been noted on any prehistoric logboat, to date.

Washstrakes There are a number of early logboats that have horizontal holes worked through their sides, near the top edge – this may be where overlapping washstrakes had formerly been fastened. However, apart from the Hasholme boat, washstrakes have not yet been found with any European prehistoric logboat. From the early centuries AD, on the other hand, there are some logboats with several added strakes such that they might appear to be planked boats: for example, *Bjorke* of 340-530 AD and *Utrecht 1 c.*885 AD.

Stabilizing timbers No prehistoric logboat has irrefutable signs of having had stabilisers fitted along its waterline. The only known British medieval logboat with them is the *c.*1300 AD Kentmere boat.

Paired logboats Paired boats are also difficult to identify among prehistoric remains, but it may be that *Clifton 1 & Clifton 2* (dated *c.*300 BC), from the River Trent near Nottingham, were such a pair: the upper sides of these boats did not survive but they were recovered from the same site and were similar in size and shape. Caesar (*DBG* 1.12) tells us that the Celtic *Helvetii* used paired boats (possibly logboats) to cross the River Saône in the first century BC. In the recent past, paired logboats were still being used in that region.

BRONZE & IRON AGE PLANK BOATS

No plank boats dated to the third millennium BC or earlier have been found in Atlantic Europe, although oak planks from the period 3700 – 4000 BC have been excavated from a Cambridgeshire mortuary chamber. Moreover, Danish logboats of the third millennium BC – *Øgårde 3* and *Verup 1* – have a row of holes along the top edge of their sides through which washstrakes might have been lashed. The earliest known Atlantic Europe plank boats are ten, or so, boats of the Later Bronze Age – one from Denmark and the remainder from southern Britain (see below). Since sewn boats were used in northern

Scandinavia in post-Roman times (in some places on into the twentieth century) it may be that other prehistoric, sewn boats await excavation.

There are suggestions in Scandinavian rock art and bronze engravings, and in certain British log coffins and logboats, that there was another Bronze Age tradition of boats with prominent keels and posts, unlike those sewn-plank boats. A boat-shaped log coffin of oak, excavated in 1937 from an Early Bronze Age round barrow at Loose Howe in north-east England, has a prominent 'keel' and a 'stem' fashioned in the solid. Examination of the remains in the 1980s confirmed that these features were not natural but had been worked. Since keel and stem are both unnecessary on a logboat, they are likely to have been copied from a contemporary plank boat (or possibly from a hide boat). Two Iron Age logboats, *Poole*, of 400-180 BC, and *Holme Pierrepont 3*, of the same era, also have 'stems' shaped in the solid, at a time when there is still no evidence in Atlantic Europe of plank boats with stems.

Scandinavian rock art and bronze engravings, some ascribed to the Bronze Age, include representations of what have been claimed to be plank boats with keels. Comparable rock engravings have been noted in Spain in the vicinity of Vigo, and on rock paintings near Cadiz. Such 'diagrammatic silhouettes' are difficult to date and to interpret. The total evidence for an early Atlantic Europe tradition of plank boats with prominent keel and stems is thus not substantial, but it should be borne in mind as an indication of what may, one day, 'turn up'.

Sewn-plank boats of the Humber basin
Between 1937 and 1989, elements of four, oak (*Quercus sp.*) sewn-plank boats (*Ferriby 1, 2, 3 & 5*) were found at North Ferriby, on the Yorkshire foreshore of the Humber estuary (Fig. 3.8); in 1996, a fifth fragment came from Kilnsea on the east coast of Yorkshire, north of the Humber. Another boat was first exposed in 1888, in a former tidal creek of the Humber at Brigg in Lincolnshire; it was re-located and excavated in 1974. This find was initially called the Brigg 'raft': in fact, it is a flat-bottomed boat. The *Ferriby 5* fragment had come from a similar boat.

Ferriby boats 1, 2 & 3 and the Kilnsea fragment
The Ferriby boats are radiocarbon dated to 1905 – 1780 BC; the Kilnsea fragment is dated *c.*1770 BC. *Ferriby 1*, of which most remains were excavated, consists of the greater part of a boat's bottom planking and a fragment of one side strake. *Ferriby 2* consists of the two parts of another boat's central bottom plank; *Ferriby 3* consists of part of a third boat's outer bottom plank and a fragment of side strake.

The central plank of boat 1's bottom planking was made (like boat 2) of two lengths joined in a simple half-lap scarf. This plank was considerably thicker than its two adjoining, outer bottom planks, and would have protruded below them in the water: it was the boat's plank-keel. Its surviving end had been shaped externally and hollowed internally to form the lower bow of this boat; the other end would have been similar. The edges of the plank-keel and the two bottom planks had been cunningly shaped so that they interlocked and so that fastenings were not exposed where they could be broken when the boat 'took the ground' at a landing place. Seams between planks were packed with a moss caulking held in place by a wooden lath; they were then fastened at *c.*25 cm. intervals by individual lashings of yew (*Taxus sp.*) that had been made pliable by twisting single withies to separate the fibres. Each stitch was then wedged fast within its holes.

The bottom planks and the plank-keel were further linked by transverse timbers through holes within cleats that had been left proud along the length of each plank. *Ferriby 2* had four sets of cleat ridges through which several mortised holes had been cut; *Ferriby 1* had individually-shaped cleats. Transverse timbers through cleats not only facilitated aligning planking after the fastenings had been periodically renewed, but also helped to keep the planking tight transversely and vertically during use, and prevented individual planks over-running and thus breaking stitches when the boat first touched the shore.

The end of the lowest side strake was fashioned in two dimensions to form the bilge of the boat and also to blend with the up-curve of the plank-keel. The upper edge of this strake had been given a half-lap

110

Fig. 3.8. Ferriby boat 1 on the foreshore of the River Humber during excavation in 1946. The ruler is 60cm long.

rabbet and fastening holes had been worked along its length. A second side strake, similar to the large fragment from Caldicot in south-east Wales (see below), would have been fastened here.

A 1:10 scale model (Fig. 3.9) of the minimum reconstruction of this boat shows this to have been a flat-bottomed boat with two side strakes, suitable for estuary work and for passages up and down rivers flowing into the Humber. Such a reconstructed boat would have measured 15.4 x 2.6 x 0.70m. At a draft of 0.30 m she could have carried crew and cargo up to *c.*3 tonnes with a freeboard of 0.40m; at 0.40m draft, 5.5 tonnes, with a freeboard of 0.30m. She would have been propelled by poles in shoal water and by paddle elsewhere, ferrying goods, animals and men within the tidal estuary and its tributaries.

E.V. Wright, the excavator of the Ferriby boats has proposed a different reconstruction which has three, rather than two, side strakes and a rockered bottom. Such a vessel would have had an enhanced performance. The inclusion of a third strake is conjectural but feasible; the rockered bottom may well be an embellishment too far.

Fig. 3.9. A model of Ferriby boat 1 after reconstruction with minimum assumptions. The parts coloured black were excavated; the remainder is conjectural.

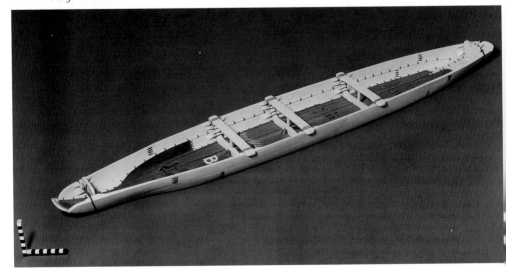

The Brigg 'raft' and Ferriby 5

The hull of this so-called 'raft' had been made watertight: it therefore was a boat, as was clearly recognised by a group of architects who visited the 1888 excavation. Their opinion was overwhelmed by the public impression that "with a flat-bottom it must be a raft". The remains were re-excavated by the National Maritime Museum, Greenwich in 1974 (Fig. 3.10 & 3.11).

The principal structural difference between this boat and Ferriby boats 1, 2 and 3 is that, while Ferriby planks were fastened together by individual yew lashings through relatively large holes, the Brigg 'raft' planking was fastened by continuous sewing of two-stranded willow (*Salix sp*) through small holes. The 'raft' also had a simpler

Fig. 3.10. A near-vertical aerial photograph of the Brigg 'raft' site during excavation in 1974. The new River Ancholme is in the foreground; North is to the left.

Fig 3.11. A vertical photograph of the Brigg 'raft' taken during photogrammetric recording.

solution to the problem of protecting the stitching from damage whenever the boat 'took the ground': its planking was, generally, thinner at the edges than elsewhere, thus the sewing (which was close to those edges) was well above the bottom of the boat. The outer edges of the Brigg outer bottom planks were not shaped but left thick, and the lowest side strakes were fastened there by continuous sewing that emerged through the outer edge of, rather than underneath, the outer bottom plank. As in the Ferriby boats, transverse timbers linked the Brigg bottom planking through mortised holes in cleats, but those cleats were bigger and spaced more closely and regularly than those on *Ferriby 1* and *Ferriby 2*. The fragment of Brigg's lower side strake that survived had fastening holes along its upper edge, a second side strake would have been fastened to it in a bevel-lap joint.

With near-vertical ends to this boat, it would originally have resembled a rectangular box without a lid, measuring 12.20 x 2.27 x 0.34-0.55m (Fig. 3.12). The 'raft' was a poled and paddled ferry across the 'Ancholme' creek at Brigg which was not only the shortest water crossing between the Lincoln Edge to the west and the Lincolnshire Wolds to the east, but also near the head of tide. This ferry could have carried loads such as twenty-six sheep and four men (draft 0.25m; freeboard 0.09m) or, with a second side-strake, seventeen cattle and six men (draft 0.46m; freeboard 0.09m). She would have played an important part in the economic and social life of North Lincolnshire. Similar flat-bottomed ferries are used today across the River Vistula in Poland (Fig. 3.13).

Ferriby 5 fragment was part of a cleat very similar in size and shape to the Brigg cleats. The original boat probably came to grief somewhere in the Humber estuary or its feeder rivers. The varying but

Fig. 3.12. A 1:10 reconstruction model of the Brigg 'raft'. The parts excavated are outlined in white.

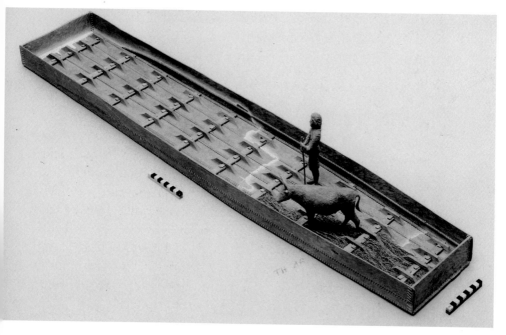

Fig. 3.13. A late-20th century ferry across the River Vistula in Poland. (Jerzy Litwin)

persistent ebbs and flows of this estuary could have deposited other fragments of the wreck almost anywhere in that tidal region. The remains found at Kilnsea were also probably from a boat that had been wrecked within the Humber estuary: a fragment subsequently drifted out of the Humber to the North Sea coast of Holderness.

Sewn-plank boats of the Severn Estuary
In 1990 and 1992, sewn plank boat fragments were excavated from two sites in the Severn Estuary. At Caldicot: a substantial oak plank fragment and another minor fragment were excavated from the former bed of the River Naddern, a tributary of the River Severn. At Goldcliff: two small fragments were excavated from the tidal foreshore of the Severn Estuary, east of the River Usk.

116

The substantial oak plank fragment (dated *c*.1785 BC) excavated at Caldicot Castle was 3.55m long, maximum breadth 0.66m and thickness varying from 60 to 90mm: the remains of three cleats protruded from its inboard face The average spacing of its fastening holes, was 0.35m indicating that individual lashings (like Ferriby) had been used, rather than continuous sewing. These were large holes suggesting that this strake would have been well above the boat's waterline, probably at the end of a second side strake of a boat that was generally like *Ferriby 1*. A narrow third strake would have been lashed to the upper edge of the Caldicot strake, in a butt joint. In this configuration (Fig. 3.14), cleats on the inboard face would have housed side timbers, as in the Dover boat (see below).

The date and the size of the fastening holes (5-8mm) on another Caldicot fragment of planking, dated to *c*.1100 BC, suggest that it was an outer section of a plank similar to the bottom planking of the Brigg

Fig. 3.14 Composite reconstruction drawing: a Ferriby outer-bottom plank and lowest side-strake with a Caldicot second side-strake and a hypothetical third side-strake.

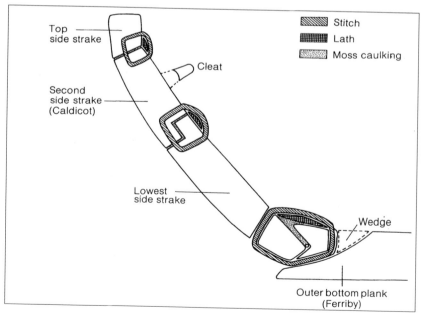

117

'raft'. Two minor fragments of oak planking, re-used on the Goldcliff foreshore as part of a 'platform', also probably came from a Brigg-style boat. Dated (unusually) by dendrochronology to c.1000 BC, both fragments had the remains of an integral cleat ridge (as on the Dover boat) with mortised holes at 0.50m interval. Holes along an edge were similar in size and spacing to those on the Brigg 'raft'.

The Dover sewn-plank boat

A sizeable proportion – two bottom planks and two lowest side strakes – of an oak sewn-plank boat, dated to c.1550 BC, was excavated from a former channel of the River Stour at Dover in 1992. Like the Ferriby boats, the Dover boat had her planking lashed together and transverse timbers through cleats linked the two bottom planks with a similar arrangement between the two side strakes (Fig. 3.15).There are other features not found in the Ferriby boats. *Dover* has a central seam (without sewn fastenings) along which her two bottom planks are butted together, edge to edge, with a moss caulking between them held in place by a lath. The two bottom planks were linked together by tapered, transverse timbers wedged within mortised holes through cleat ridges ('rails') fashioned along the inner edges of both planks. Another unique feature is that the ends of the inner ridges on the two *Dover* bottom planks splay outwards into a yoke shape. Holes through this yoke would formerly have been where a (missing) end-closing timber (a transom board?) was fastened and held in place by wedges.

Efforts to produce a hypothetical reconstruction of this boat seem to have been driven by a desire to ensure that it would be capable of seagoing passages, and a belief that, since it was found at Dover, it must have been used there as a cross-Channel ferry. Palaeo-environmental research indicates that, in the Bronze Age, the River Dour was a shallow, braided stream and was therefore unsuitable for this boat. That the remains were deposited at Dover may be explained by considering another area within this region where such a boat is likely to have been used. The ancient Watsum Channel, between Kent and the Isle of Thanet, was comparable, in several ways, with the Humber Estuary. Moreover, ferries were used to cross to and from the

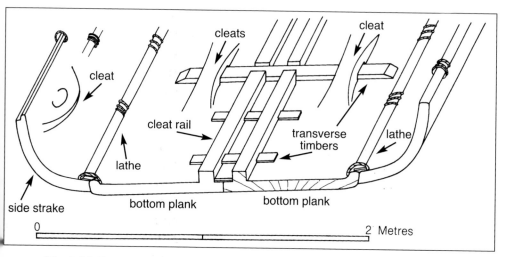

Fig. 3.15. Diagram illustrating the structure of the Dover Boat.

Isle of Thanet from early Neolithic times until the late-medieval period when the channel became fully-silted. It is intrinsically more likely that it was a Watsum Channel ferry, rather than a Dover Straight boat that was wrecked at Dover. After such a disaster, fragments could have drifted southwards from the Watsum Channel and eventually deposited at Dover. Comparable reasoning probably explains how the Kilnsea boat fragment was deposited on the Yorkshire coast, north of Spurn Point rather than that boat's usual operating region within the Humber Estuary.

British sewn plank boats
In addition to the sewn-plank boat remains from the Humber and Severn estuaries described above, there is a minor fragment from the Testwood valley, near Southampton, dated *c.*1100 BC. The abandoned or wrecked boats, that those eleven groups of remains now represent, had several features in common: they were built in the plank-first sequence; plank seams were caulked by moss held in place by longitudinal laths; substantial oak planks were fastened together by individual lashings or by running sewing; the bottom planking was

linked together by transverse timbers and the side planking by side timbers, both sets of timbers being wedged within cleats that were integral with the planking; special woodworking techniques were used to ensure that, when these boats took the ground (as they frequently did), the plank fastenings were not damaged; and those finds that can be reconstructed were narrow, relatively long boats with a L/B ratio of 6-8:1.

These finds may be divided into two groups by reference to their date and their plank fastenings:

Group A: *Ferriby 1, 2 & 3, Dover, Caldicot 1* (and probably *Kilnsea*). These boats, from *c.*2000 to 1500 BC (Earlier Bronze Age), had interlocking, edge-to-edge or half-lap planking fastened together by individual lashings using sizeable cords through large holes (25-35mm diameter). Dover also had wedges through cleat rails as bottom plank fastenings.

Group B: Brigg 'raft', *Caldicot 2, Goldcliff,* (and probably *Ferriby 5* and *Testwood*).
These boats, from *c.*1100 to 500 BC (Later Bronze Age), had edge-to-edge and bevel-lap planking fastened together by running stitching through small holes (*c.*10mm diameter).

Scandinavian Sewn-Plank Boats
Sewn plank boats have also been excavated in Scandinavia: there are finds from the fourth century BC to the fourth century AD in Denmark, Sweden and Norway, moreover, even when iron nails began to be used as plank fastenings, from the fourth century AD, frames/ribs continued to be lashed in position. The Barset boat of the eighth century AD was almost entirely built clinker-fashion, but its top strake was fastened with sewing and intermittent treenails.

Tentative evidence for lashings used as plank fastenings comes from Danish logboats of the fourth millennium BC which seem to have had washstrakes lashed to their top edges. Repairs in second millennium BC logboats are the earliest evidence for what may have been running sewing in Scandinavia. In 1921-2 a sewn plank boat was excavated from Hjortspring, a former lake on the island of Als in southern Denmark. In outline, this boat resembled boats depicted on some Scandinavian rock carvings and on certain Bronze Age swords. The main structural parts of this boat were lime (*Tilia sp.*): her planking was sewn together and her transverse timbers were lashed to cleats integral with that planking.

The slightly-hollowed, bottom plank was extended at both ends by an up-curving timber that formed a lower 'beak'. Block stems hewn to shape, stood on the bottom plank and were sewn to it near each end using cord of two-ply birch or fir roots; the fastening holes were plugged with an animal fat and linseed mix. The two block stems were each extended by a timber which became the upper 'beak'. The characteristic form of the boat's ends was completed by adding two vertical timbers one of which locked the upper 'beak' to the lower 'beak'; the other locked the upper 'beak' to the bottom plank.

The planking (two each side) was sewn to the wings of the block stems, to each other and to the bottom plank in bevelled laps giving the boat a smooth 'skin'. The framing, consisting of pre-stressed hazel (*Corylus sp.*) ribs, upper crossbeam/thwarts, lower crossbeams and vertical ash (*Fraxinus sp.*) timbers, was so interlocked that it would have had to be assembled before being lashed to cleats left proud of the planking, thereby forcing the planking together (Fig. 3.16).

Fig. 3.16. The conserved framing of the Hjortspring boat, re-assembled.

The Hjortspring boat was propelled by twenty paddlers, two to each thwart, with a steersman at bow and stern. She measured (without projections) c.13.61 x 2.04 x 0.71m. Having smooth planking, a low volumetric coefficient and L/B ratio of 10:1, she would have had a good turn of speed in fair conditions. She is dated 350 – 300 BC.

Prehistoric seafaring

The movement of ideas, and probably of people, becomes archaeologically visible as 'monuments', 'rituals' or technological innovations. These, together with direct evidence from exotic goods, can be interpreted as evidence for sea passages to or from islands. Unless there is evidence to the contrary, it should be assumed that between islands, or between an island and a continent, the shortest sea crossing was taken, if for no other reason than that sail was unknown in north-west Europe until the sixth century BC, and boats would have been paddled or under oars.

The shortest overseas route between Britain and Ireland would have been across the North Channel, but it may be that the longer route from Anglesey to Dublin Bay, although lengthy, may have been practicable since, in days of good visibility, the mountains of one land can be seen before losing contact with the other. Between England and France, the Dover strait crossing would, have been, by far, the shortest. Both these routes were crossings on which visual pilotage techniques would have been used. After such a crossing from Britain to France, a succession of short-haul passages, generally in sight of land, could have been made in coastal waters sheltered by a series of islands, taking craft as far north as Norway or as far south as Spain.

It is difficult to say when long distance, direct overseas routes from and to Britain became possible. In the South Pacific and also in the Mediterranean (see p.49–51) the art and science of navigating out-of-sight of land seems to have been acquired by the mid-second millennium BC. Sometime between then and the Roman period it seems likely that open sea crossings began to be used in Atlantic Europe.

Most of the early boats so far excavated in Britain were lake and river boats: some few others (sewn-plank boats) would have been useable in estuaries and, except on rare occasions of settled weather, would not have been sea-going. This is not because they were sewn plank boats: there are many recent counter examples. Rather, it is because their size, shape and structure would have meant that they would have had insufficient stability, freeboard and sea-keeping qualities for such a role. In the absence of a known seagoing boat, a hypothetical Bronze Age hide boat with a prominent keel, a wicker framing and a hull shape convenient to paddlers (see p.101). may be considered. Alternatively, the even more hypothetical, Bronze Age plank boat with a keel and a prominent stem (see p.109) could be a candidate.

VESSELS BUILT MEDITERRANEAN FASHION

A handful of vessels excavated in north-west Europe had been built Mediterranean-style, with locked mortise and tenon plank fastenings. The County Hall ship, excavated from a site near the River Thames in London in 1910-11 and dated to AD 295, was built almost entirely in that Roman manner, but dendrochronology shows that she was built of oak from the south-east of England. This ship may well have been a ferry between Britain and the Continent, as also may some of the Romano-Celtic boats discussed below. Professor Barry Cunliffe has shown that much of the first century BC trade between the Mediterranean and north-west Europe was up the Rhône or the Aude and down the Garonne, Loire, Seine or Rhine; then northwards along the Atlantic coast. Nevertheless, Portuguese amphorae have been excavated from Vindolanda in northern Britain. Moreover, during the Roman period, a lighthouse was built at La Coruña in north-west Spain, a vital landmark for ships: this must mean that they were relatively frequent on this route by that time (see p.89). Moreover, it is not impossible that, by that date, direct crossings of the Bay of Biscay, from Coruña to Ushant, were undertaken, rather than a coastal passage along the French lee shore.

Other vessels with mortise and tenon plank fastenings include three first to second century AD boats excavated in the Low Countries: one from Vechten in 1893 and two from Zwammerdam (boats *2A & 6*) in

1968-1971. Such fastenings were also used to join together parts of a Zwammerdam steering oar. Two riverboats from a Danube site at Oberstimm in central Germany were also built 'in the Classical manner'. During Caesar's campaign in Gaul (*DBG* 3.9.1) he had warships built on the River Loire. It seems likely that these ships were built Mediterranean fashion as they were said to be different from the ships of the Veneti.

An extended logboat, excavated from Lough Lene in County Westmeath, Ireland, and dated to the third or fourth centuries AD, had oak washstrakes fastened, edge-to-edge, to its logboat base by mortise and tenon joints. Similar fastenings found on boat planking re-used as coffins in Vietnam, illustrate the wide spread of Roman boatbuilding methods – from 7°W to 110°E and 53°N to 15°N.

ROMANO-CELTIC VESSELS

Two first century AD, bronze coins issued by Cunobelin of the Catavellauni in south-east Britain feature a ship propelled by a square sail set on a midships mast, and steered by a side rudder. A protruding forefoot, a spar at the stem head, possibly for a bowline, and braces to each yardarm suggest a bid for weatherly performance. Caesar (*DBG* 3.13 – see also Strabo: 4.4.1.) – noted that the Veneti of western France had seagoing sailing ships that were solidly built, more seaworthy and better suited to the seas of the Channel than were Caesar's own ships: they could not only sail closer inshore, but also take the ground readily in those difficult tidal waters. The Veneti ships had flush-laid, oak planking, caulked with 'seaweed' (moss?), that were fastened to one foot (0.30m) thick framing timbers by iron nails, one inch (25mm) in shank diameter. They were propelled by leather sails and used on coastal passages and on cross-Channel voyages to Britain.

A group of twenty-five to thirty wrecks, excavated in the Severn estuary, the Thames at London, off Guernsey, and in the Schelde/Meuse/Rhine delta, the Rhine at Xanten and at Mainz, and in the Swiss Lake Neuchâtel, have several of the features noted by Caesar. This boatbuilding tradition is now known as 'Romano-Celtic':

'Romano' reflects the temporal range, from first to fourth century AD and acknowledges the possibility of some Roman technological influence: for example, the use of saws to fashion planking ; 'Celtic' because of their spatial distribution in regions that were, or had been, occupied by Celtic-speaking peoples.

Some of those finds have not yet been published in detail. Nevertheless, the main body of vessels in this polythetic group generally have these distinctive features:

- the framing of relatively massive and closely-spaced timbers, includes floors spanning bottom and bilges, asymmetric timbers (half-frames) spanning the bottom and a side, and side timbers; there may be more than one timber at a station, but individual timbers are not fastened together.
- flush-laid planking is fastened to that framework by relatively large iron nails (sometimes driven through treenails) clenched by turning ('hooked') the emerging point back through 180° (Fig. 3.17).
- planking is caulked within seams, using macerated wooden twigs, twisted fibres or moss.
- hulls are either: flat-bottomed, keel-less and without posts ('barge-like'); or full-bodied with a firm bilge and with posts and a plank-keel.
- the mast step (towing and/or sailing) is well-forward of amidships.

These vessels may be divided into two groups identified principally by hull shape (and therefore, function) and the presence or absence of a plank-keel:

Barge-like boats, (Type A)
These were flat-bottomed and keel-less, with a 'box-like' transverse section, and without posts (Fig. 3.18). They were used on the rivers, canals and lakes of the greater Rhine region, towed, or propelled by paddle, pole or oar. Examples are the boats from Bevaix, Zwammerdam and Pommeroeul. Several boats excavated at Mainz,

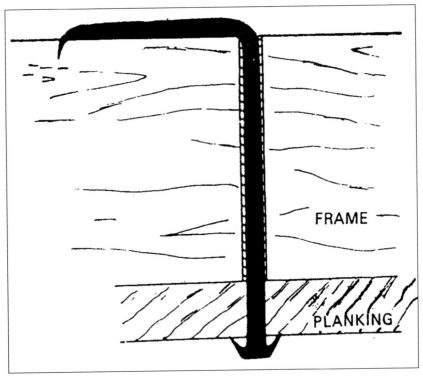

Fig. 3.17. A hooked nail fastening plank to frame in Blackfriars boat 1. (after Marsden)

although from the Rhine, had hulls similar in some respects to the hulls of the seagoing vessels in Type B: this may be due to their military, rather than cargo-carrying, function. There is more variability in Type A boats, and more adoption of Roman practices, than in Type B. Moreover not all are recorded and published to a uniformly high standard.

Seagoing vessels (Type B)
With plank-keels and posts, these vessels had a full-bodied transverse section with a firm bilge and were propelled by sail in estuaries and on seagoing passages. Vessels in this group are: the mid-second century *Blackfriars 1* from the River Thames at London; the late third

Fig 3.18. A Romano-Celtic river 'barge' during excavation at Zwammerdam, the
Netherlands.

Fig. 3.19. The Romano-Celtic boat from Barland's Farm during excavation in 1993.

century *St Peter Port 1* from Guernsey and the AD 300 estuary and coastal boat from Barland's Farm (Fig. 3.19) in south-east Wales, on the northern shores of the River Severn. A late second century AD boat, partly-excavated in 1958 from the New Guy's House site near the River Thames in London, may also be a member of this group. More research is needed before the relationship between Type A and Type B vessels can be fully understood.

Sequence of building
The Barland's Farm vessel (Fig. 3.20) was built in the frame-first sequence: framing was erected on the plank-keel and posts, and the planking was then fastened to it. At stage 4 in the building sequence illustrated in Fig 1.2, this boat's hull was clearly outlined by posts, plank-keel, floor timbers and half-frames, before any planking had been added.

It seems likely that those elements of the Barland's Farm boat's framework that defined her hull shape were initially 'designed by eye'. Using inherited wisdom, his own expertise, and possibly details from another boat, the builder would have fashioned plank-keel, posts and some of the framing, and set them up (Fig. 3.21). The hull form thus displayed would have been refined by shaping the outer faces of frames until ribbands (a pair of temporary splines) from post to post confirmed that fair curves had been achieved, and the builder's eye told him that this shape would give the hull form that he had in mind. From such beginnings, simple ratios and rules of thumb may well have been developed so that, using ribbands, a successful 'design' could be repeated. The ratio of the maximum beam of the Barland's Farm boat, to her length of plank-keel, to length overall seems to have been 1:2:3.

Fig. 3.20. A 1:10 'as-found' model of the Barland's Farm boat incorporating representations of all timbers excavated.

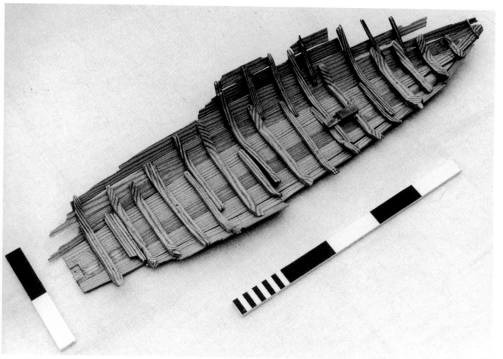

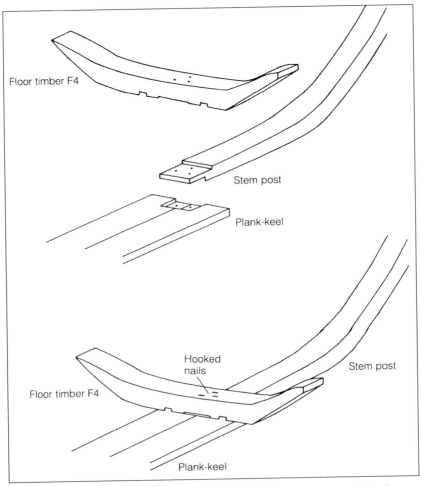

Fig. 3.21. Diagram showing the Barland's Farm joint between plank-keel, stern post and floor F4.

Moreover, units of measurement (0.55m and 0.56m) have been identified in the frame spacing of the Barland's boat and the St Peter Port ship: these intervals were probably the length of two human feet or, possibly, an 'ell' measured from elbow to fingertip. This unit may also have been used to obtain the curve of her lower post and the curved ends of her framing timbers.

130

Since *St Peter Port 1* and *Blackfriars 1* were bigger than the Barland's Farm boat, they had no single element of framework that defined the shape of their hulls from plank-keel to sheer-line. The shape of the upper hull of these two ships had therefore to come in a second phase when side timbers were fastened to their fourth strakes and extended upwards to the sheerline. Rather than the 'frame-first' sequence of the Barland's boat, *Blackfriars 1* and *St Peter Port 1* were built in the 'framing first' sequence: first, some framing, then the lower hull planking; next more framing, then upper hull planking.

The origin of 'frame-first'?

Of the three frame-first/framing-first vessels now known in north-west Europe, *Blackfriars 1*, from the second century AD, is the earliest. The earliest–known frame-first Mediterranean vessel is dated to the sixth century AD (see p.84). That difference in dates makes it likely that the idea of using the frame-first building sequence originated within north-west Europe where the hide-boat building sequence, with its use of a framework to control the hull shape, would have been familiar.

Tools and Techniques

Some Roman tools and techniques – for example, sawn planking – were used when building those Romano-Celtic vessels. Hooked bronze nails had been used to fasten frames to planking in the Mediterranean from *c*.400 BC; on the other hand, turned and hooked iron nails were used in northern Europe in the manufacture of cart wheels during Halstatt times, before 500 BC. Thus it is possible that the hooked iron nails used to fasten planking to framing in Romano-Celtic vessels was an indigenous northern European technique. If, as seems likely, hide boats were built centuries (possibly millennia) before plank boats, the builders of the first Blackfriars-style, frame-first (or framing-first) boat would have known of that hide boat building sequence and could have used it.

Group B characteristics

The three members of Group B were estuary/seagoing vessels. When hypothetically reconstructed, *Blackfriars 1* measured *c*.18.5 x 6.12 x 2.86m; *St Peter Port 1*, *c*.25 x 6 x 3m and the Barland's Farm boat, *c.*11.4 x 3.16 x 0.90m – the third one was clearly a boat; the other two may be called 'ships'. The three have L/B ratios of 3-4: 1; L/D ratios 6.6-8.3: 1 (ships); 12.7: 1 (boat). All three have plank-keels: *St Peter Port*'s was made of three-planks laid side-by-side; the others, of two planks. These keels protruded below the bottom planking to reduce leeway, yet these vessels were able to take the ground in tidal waters and sit there in a near-vertical state. The ships have a full-bodied transverse section with a firm bilge; the boat is flat in the floors and has curved, flaring sides. The ships would have been sea-going in the Channel region; the boat was suited for passages within the central and eastern Bristol Channel, the Severn Estuary and the many rivers flowing into it.

All three vessels have a mast step at approximately one-third the waterline length from the bow: the ships, in a floor timber, the boat, in a short fore-and-aft timber. All three were sailing, cargo vessels: the boat could additionally be propelled by oars. Their sawn, oak planking was flush-laid, edge-to-edge with butts at frame stations. A caulking of macerated wood with tar or resin was tacked or 'glued' to plank edges before the next plank was fastened at each frame station by hook-clenched nails. The ships had iron nails that were up to 80cm in length; the nails in the Barland's Farm boat were 10-25cm long.

At a draft of 0.34m, with a crew of three, The Barland's boat could have carried *c.*4.5 tonnes of cargo; at 0.52m draft (60% height of sides) she could have carried *c.*6.5 tonnes. At an estimated 60% draft, *Blackfriars 1* could have carried 63.7 tonnes.

Propulsion and Steering

The Group A boats were propelled by oar, pole or by being towed. All three Group B vessels had mast steps set about one-third the waterline length of the vessel from the bow (Fig. 3.22); a mast is shown stepped in this position on the first century AD monument for Blussus. To obtain sail balance on a mast in this position and to achieve windward performance, a fore-and-aft sail such as a lug would have to be set. On the other hand, the masts on the first century BC gold model from Broighter (Fig. 3.3), in the north of Ireland, and on the first century

Fig. 3.22. A 1:10 reconstruction model of the Barland's Farm boat with a conjectural lugsail. (Newport Museum)

AD Cunobelin coins from Canterbury and Colchester, were all stepped amidships. It may be that, from the second century AD, mast steps on Celtic craft were moved forward to match a fore-and-aft sail rather than a square sail.

Steering oars have been excavated at Bruges, Zwammerdam and Neuchâtel, associated, directly or indirectly, with Romano-Celtic boats. They were also depicted on the Blussus monument and on a first century AD altar to Nehellannia from Colijnsplaat in the Netherlands, and one was part of the Broighter model boat's equipment. Metal terminals for poles have been excavated from Roman period sites in the Rhine region.

Celtic seafaring

An extract from a sixth century BC periplus (sailing directions), incorporated by fourth century AD Avienus in his *Ora Maritima*, describes how Celtic people of Brittany sailed to Ireland in two days, passing in sight of Britain on the way. Pliny (*NH* 4. 104) of the first century AD, quoting Timaeus' early third century BC history, noted that Britons were involved in similar, overseas trading voyages, and Caesar (*DBG* 3.13), of the first century BC, described the seagoing ships in which the Veneti of south-west Brittany traded with Britain.

Once the pattern of the tides is understood, tidal ebbs and flows can be used to advantage, taking boats well inland, up rivers, and then back down again. In addition to cross-Channel passages, classical authors mention the Bay of Biscay and southern North Sea trade routes as far north as the Rhine/Thames crossing. Many of the landing places associated with those routes may not be now recognisable since, not only were they informal beach landings within natural harbours with little, or no, man-made structures, but also because of subsequent changes in sea level.

Although all such sea crossings would begin and end with pilotage techniques when land was in sight, the middle section of almost every route was out-of-sight of land, and non-instrumental navigation had to be undertaken. On passages between Brittany and south-east Ireland, and from Brittany to Cornwall, land would have been out-of-sight for a considerable time. Even on mid-Channel routes to Poole and Portsmouth harbours, there would have been a minimum of ten nautical miles when land was invisible (even in good weather), and on Rhine/Thames passages, this distance would have been thirty to forty miles because of the low-lying coastal terrain on both shores.

The non-instrumental navigational techniques used on those out–of-sight-of-land stretches would have been generally similar to those used in the Mediterranean and elsewhere, but the Atlantic seaman would also have had to take account not only of tides and tidal flows, but also of weather forecasting since there would have been greater, and more frequent, cloud cover than in the Mediterranean restricting the use of celestial methods of navigation. The Celtic apprentice seaman would have had much to learn from his seniors, but stereotyped phrases and rules of thumb would have assisted memory. Ceasar (*DBG* VI. 14) noted that the Celts paid great attention to memory training for the transmission of learning and culture: moreover, they studied the motion of the stars and related topics, with particular emphasis on the moon – a practice that would have been invaluable when forecasting tides and tidal flows and keeping the reckoning when out-of-sight of land.

BOATS AND SHIPS OF THE 1ST MILLENNIUM A.D.
The Nordic Tradition – fourth to tenth century AD
Overlapping planking became a primary feature of the Nordic tradition of boat and ship-building, but a form of it was used much earlier. Moreover, two Danish logboats of the third millennium BC (*Øgarde 3* and *Verup 1*) may have had overlapping washstrakes. Later, but before the Viking Age, examples with a bevelled lap (overlapping, but with the appearance of being flush-laid) include:

- side strakes were lashed/sewn to the strake below in a bevelled-lap on the *Dover* and *Ferriby 1* boats of the early to mid-second millennium BC, and on the Brigg 'raft' of the early first millennium BC;
- the planking of the Hjortspring boat, of 350-300 BC, was fastened

together in a bevelled-lap;
• washstrakes on the Hasholme logboat of *c.*300BC were fastened in a half-lap joint to a rabbet along the upper, outer edge of the logboat hull to form a 'ship-lap' joint by treenails driven from outboard and locked inboard by wooden keys (cotters);
• west Norwegian boats from Valerøy (*c.*AD 245) and Halsnøy (*c.* AD 335) had overlapping planking sewn together outside the lap.

The oldest-known clinker planking fastened within the overlap, (similar to that which became known as '*Viking*') appears to be that of the fragmented *Nydam boat 1* recently dated to *c.*AD 200; another early example of clinker planking is the washstrake fastened to a Swedish extended logboat from Bjorke, of *c.*AD 340-530. Around the same date, and also with a visible overlap, were several Romano-Celtic boats: *Pommeroel 5*, *Woerdan* and *Zwammerdam 2 & 5* – all from the Low Countries: their strakes were fastened together with iron nails that were turned, rather than clenched by deformation.

The Nydam boats

Three clinker-built boats were excavated in 1863 from a former freshwater lake at Nydam on the east coast of Jutland, only six miles from Hjortspring (see p.121–122). Like the Bjorke boat, these boats had overlapping planking fastened together within the overlap by clenched iron nails. Furthermore, their framing was lashed to cleats integral with the planking. Boat 1 had been broken up. Boat 3, with mainly pine planking, had lime top strakes lashed or sewn on by lime bast rope – this boat was destroyed during the Prussia and Denmark war. Boat 2, slightly damaged, survived almost entirely and is now displayed in Schleswig (Fig.3.23). This boat had several structural features that were to become characteristic of the Nordic boat and ship-building tradition that blossomed between the ninth and eleventh centuries AD.

Nydam 2 was re-assessed in the late twentieth century by Roskilde's Institute of Maritime Archaeology: their examination confirmed that bottom boards, fastened together by lime bast cord,

Fig. 3.23. Nydam 2 on display in the Schleswig-Holstein Landesmuseum, Germany.

were supported on horizontal poles, and showed that much of the upper planking, the framing and all the rowlocks had been replaced after excavation. Dendro-chronology dated the felling of the oaks from which this boat had been built to AD 310-320. This large, double-ended, open-boat has a plank-keel to which both stems were scarfed in a horizontal lap fastened by treenails. Her oak planking had been fastened together by clenched iron nails; the top strake, being appreciably thicker than the others, contributed to the hull's integrity. Planks within strakes range in length from 8 to 12m. Frames run from near-sheer to near-sheer, and are spaced at *c.*1m apart; they are lashed to cleats proud of the planking. Thwarts/crossbeams take against frame heads and are supported by pillars. There would have been fifteen oarsmen each side: two on each thwart, each man working his oar against a curved thole timber lashed to the top strake.

The boat now measures 23.7 x 3.75 x 1.20m: over the 125, or so, years since excavation her planks have shrunk in breadth so that the depth of hull would originally have been greater. This boat would have been steered by a side rudder similar to one recently excavated that is believed to have belonged to *Nydam 3*. There was no sign of propulsion by sail on any of these boats.

Seventh century boats

Nydam 2 was bigger and stronger than the Hjortspring boat, and further size increase occurred during the seventh century, as seen in vessels excavated at Kongesgärde on the east coast of Jutland, Gretstedbro on the west; Kvalsund in Sunmøre, Norway; and three ship burials in eastern England – two at Sutton Hoo and one at Snape. Those three ship burials survived as fragile impressions in the soil: casts of frames lay across impressions of planks with highly corroded fastenings (Fig. 3.24).

Several of the embryonic Nordic features found in *Nydam boat 2* were also in those seventh century vessels. Other features were changed: planks became narrower and shorter, possibly because boatbuilders found that the required hull shapes could best be formed by shorter planks, or it may be that tall oaks were no longer available. Other changes were that tholes were spiked, rather than lashed, to the top strake and, although some seventh century vessel continued to have lashed framing, others were fastened by treenails with a few fastened by iron nails.

There was no evidence for the use of sail in any of these vessels, yet sail had been used by seagoing boats in the British and Irish archipelago since at least the first century BC and probably as early as the sixth century BC (see p.132–4). In Scandinavia the earliest evidence for sail appears in the seventh century AD in vessels on Gotland memorial stones depicted with a square sail on a mast stepped amidships.

Ninth to tenth century vessels

Late ninth century voyages by Ohthere, along the northern coast of Norway, and by Wulfstan in the Baltic, illustrate that, by this time, there was widespread use of sail in Scandinavian waters, probably in

Fig. 3.24. Sutton Hoo 2 surviving as an impression in the sandy soil, during excavation in 1939. (The British Museum)

ships similar to the Norwegian Klåstad ship and the Swedish Äskekärr ship, both of the tenth century. Three other sailing ships, all of them built of oak, were excavated in Norway during the late nineteenth/early twentieth century: the Oseberg ship of AD 815-820 (Figs 3.25); the Gokstad ship of *c.*895, and Tune of AD 910-920. Professor Christensen has interpreted these ships as 'typical, non-specialised, Early Viking Age ships used for war, trade or prestige, as occasion arose'.

As the Oseberg ship now stands on display at Bygdøy near Oslo (Fig. 3.26), with some of her timbers and fastenings replaced, her principal features are a guide to the original, early-ninth century ship. She measures 22 x 5.2 x 1.6m, with L/B ratio of 4.2:1 and L/D of 13.75:1. High, curving stems were fastened to her T-section keel in vertical scarfs. Twelve slim strakes each side are fastened together in what had by then become standard clinker fashion. The tenth strakes,

Fig. 3.25. The early-9th century Oseberg ship exposed within her burial mound in 1904.

Fig. 3.26. The Oseberg ship, restored and on display in the museum at Bigdøy, Oslo.

with an inverted-L cross section similar to the top strakes of *Nydam 2*, are transition strakes between bottom and sides; this change is emphasised by discontinuity in the hull's transverse section. These two thick, waterline strakes, subsequently known as *meginhufr* ('strong strake'), not only distributed sailing stresses around the hull, but also, in conjunction with the keel and the thickened top strake, increased the longitudinal strength of the hull.

Naturally-grown floor timbers, spaced at *c.*1m apart and symmetrical about the ship's centre line, are not fastened to the keel

141

but are lashed to cleats on her first eight strakes, using baleen strips, with their upper ends nailed to the ninth strake. Across the heads of each floor, at tenth strake level, there are crossbeams rabbeted to take bottom boards. The eleventh and twelfth strakes are supported by nail-fastened, grown knees. Strengthened framing on the starboard quarter supported the side rudder held to the frame by a flexible withy rope and a plaited leather band.

A keelson with a mast step spans two floors near amidships; above it is a mast partner that spans four beams. Near contemporary ship depictions suggest that Oseberg would have set a square sail on a mast that had a forestay and shrouds, possibly with a bowline to the sail's luff (weather edge).

Changes between sixth/seventh century and the tenth century

Between the seventh century (Sutton Hoo – an oared vessel) and the early ninth century (Oseberg – sailed), the relative depth of hull was increased from an L/D of 18-20:1 to 13.75:1, and relative breadth from an L/B of 6:1 to 4.2:1. These changes gave the extra stability and freeboard required by the adoption of sail. That increased freeboard led to a change from rowlocks above the sheer strake to oar ports through that strake; it also meant that crossbeams, being lower, could no longer be used as thwarts: it is assumed that, instead, seaman's chests were used by oarsmen.

A short keelson was introduced to act as mast step and a mast partner provided further support to the mast at crossbeam height. The garboard strakes were given a greater deadrise (from 16° to 31°), and the ship's midship section became more V-shaped than rounded. The keel changed from a plank-keel to a foil-shaped, plank-on-edge keel protruding deeper into the sea, thereby minimising leeway.

Eighty years or so after Oseberg, the Gokstad and Tune ships of the early-tenth century still had Oseberg's distinctive, general hull form and many of her structural features. Improvements were made by giving the *meginhufr* of the later ships a more wedge-shaped section, leading to a smoother transition between bottom and sides. There were other changes in details, many of them aimed at improving sailing performance: Gokstad had three pairs of rigging cleats aft, and the heel of a tacking boom (*beitiass*) fitted into sockets in wooden blocks treenailed to the planking, thus keeping the luff of the sail taut. With sixteen strakes, including two strakes above her oarport strake, and an L/D ratio of 10.9:1, Gokstad had greater freeboard than Oseberg (with only twelve strakes); she also had oarport lids. In longitudinal profile, Gokstad did not have Oseberg's exaggerated sheer at the ends, thereby reducing windage and leeway. Furthermore, Gokstad's mast was nearer amidships than Oseberg's, giving a better balance between hull and rig, and her keelson, braced by knees, spanned four frames compared with Oseberg's two.

Early cargo ships and warships
The tenth century Klåstad ship was generally similar in structure and in shape to the Gokstad ship but she had a *meginhufr* similar to that of Oseberg which gave her a marked discontinuity in transverse section. The lower frames of the Tune and Gokstad ships were lashed to cleats on their planking and their upper frames were treenailed: Klåstad frames were all treenailed. The Klåstad ship was carrying whetstone blanks on a dunnage of hazel sticks and it has been claimed that she was a specialised cargo carrier. On the other hand, her general proportions are mid-way between Oseberg and Gokstad: this suggests that she was, like her predecessors, a 'general-purpose' ship.

The tenth century Äskekärr ship, on the other hand, was relatively deeper and broader than earlier ships and had a more rectangular transverse section (high block coefficient) and thus her hold had a greater volume. That she probably had a second level of crossbeams at the twelfth strake (out of thirteen) strengthens the possibility that she was a specialised cargo ship.

Two ships excavated from burial mounds (one late-ninth century, at Hedeby, and one mid-tenth century, at Ladby in Denmark) may have been specialised warships. The Hedeby ship had an L/B ratio of *c*.6:1; Ladby had an L/B of 6.7:1 and an L/D of 21:1. That high L/D ratio compared with L/D of 8 to15:1 for Oseberg, Gokstad, Tune, Klastad and Askekarr, and the high L/B ratios of 6 and 6.7, compared with ratios of 3.5 to 4.6 for that same range of vessels, suggest that Ladby and Hedeby had been 'designed' as speedy fighting vessels.

Vessels of the southern Baltic

Several medieval boats excavated from the southern coast of the Baltic, similar in form and structure to the early medieval Scandinavian ships discussed above, differ in a minor way, from them: instead of iron nail fastenings and a caulking of animal hair (Fig. 1.3D), they had headed and wedged treenails and moss (Fig.1.3 E). These vessels, generally less than 16m in length, include *Gdańsk-Orunia 1, 2 & 3*; *Charbrow Ralswick 2 & 4*; *Walin*; and *Fribrødre* on the island of Falster: they all seem suitable for use on rivers and lakes. Some of them also have their mast stepped in a floor timber rather than a keelson, but this may not be a defining characteristic. It has been suggested that these vessels, were an adaptation of the 'mainstream' Nordic technique by seventh to twelfth century western Slavs for whom iron was scarce and moss plentiful.

Southern North Sea region

In 1970, the remains of a late ninth century, clinker-built boat were excavated from a former tidal creek of the River Thames, at Graveney, east of Faversham in Kent. She differed from the 'standard' Nordic vessel in several ways:

Form. She was relatively broader and had a less-deep hull, and her form was fuller than the Nordic vessel – almost flat-bottomed. She had raking, overhanging ends with an angular forefoot rather than Nordic-style rising ends blending into the keel in a continuous curve.

Structure. Her floor timbers were relatively massive and much closer together than contemporary Nordic vessels. The floors were not symmetrical but L-shaped half-frames, alternating port and starboard. There were no knees, but longitudinal stringers supported frames. Her raking post had a long horizontal part joined to the keel in a horizontal, rather than vertical, scarf. She had two thickish binding strakes rather than a *meginhufr* and her plank-fastening nails were driven through treenails.

Several of these 'deviations' are probably because this boat was used to transport heavy loads within a tidal estuary, from and to beach landing places. Further explanation is required for three other features: raking posts with a prolonged horizontal element; asymmetric half-frames; and plank-fastening nails driven through treenails. These could all have been inherited from the Romano-Celtic tradition of seagoing boats and ships, as exemplified by the first to fourth century AD finds: *Blackfriars 1*, *St Peter Port 1* and the Barland's Farm boat (see p.124–134) had raking posts with a prolonged horizontal element, asymmetric half-frames (but in pairs and not joined to other timbers), and iron nails through treenails were used to fasten planking to framing (they were built frame-first). In the Classical Mediterranean, on the other hand, this fastening technique had been used (as in the Graveney boat which, like Classical vessels, was built plank-first) to fasten the planking together. In Classical and in Romano-Celtic vessels, moreover, such nails were clenched by hooking the point back into the timbers, whereas in Graveney (as in the Nordic tradition) points were deformed.

It seems likely that the Graveney boatbuilders had inherited building techniques from both Romano-Celtic and Nordic traditions. Moreover, superimposed on an amalgamation of these two sets of techniques was the local requirement that this boat should be capable of transporting heavy loads from beach landing places in the tidal Thames estuary.

The Nordic tradition

Twenty five years ago Ole Crumlin–Pedersen, the doyen of Nordic boat archaeology and renowned excavator of the Skuldelev ships (Fig. 3.27), claimed that finds of Nordic vessels were 'so numerous that it is possible to make statements about basic patterns in shipbuilding with reasonable certainty as well as discuss some of the variations'. Subsequent analyses of even more Nordic vessels have added support to Crumlin-Pedersen's assertion. His publication of the five Skuldelev

Fig. 3.27. The five, 11th century Skuldelev vessels under excavation within a coffer dam in Roskilde fjord in 1962.

vessels has clarified the 'Viking' ship's characteristic features. More has also been learnt from timbers and planking from dismantled Nordic ships reused in waterfront structures or as fill when tidal foreshores were enclosed – for example, in Bergen and Dublin. Furthermore, ships of this tradition are depicted on the eleventh/twelfth century Bayeux tapestry and, from later centuries, on town seals. From this wealth of evidence it is possible to discern the principal features of Nordic shipbuilding and to outline changes that took place in the post-Viking, late medieval period. More is known, and known in more detail, about Nordic shipbuilding, than any other ancient shipbuilding tradition in the world.

'Design'

How did the Nordic boat builder obtain the shape of hull that he wanted? Did he build entirely 'by eye'? Or were there rules of thumb, simple geometric drawings or building aids such as boat ells and boat levels, as recently used in Norway? Partly-worked stem posts have been recovered from bogs (formerly ponds) in Scandinavia and in Britain. On one such unused stem from the island of Eigg, landings for the ends of six pairs of strakes, and lines giving the run of each strake, had been scribed. Before fashioning this stem, the builder must have had in his head some idea of the shape of the hull that the stem was to fit. Crumlin-Pedersen has demonstrated how such a stem could have been fashioned. With the intended keel length as the standard unit, and using string and chalk or charcoal, a stem could be defined by several circles of radii proportionate to that keel length. Rules of thumb, as used for example, in Tamil Nadu today, could have been compiled giving specific radii for different keel lengths and for the different function intended for each boat. Professor Richard Steffy has used similar methods to investigate the 'design' of the eleventh century ship excavated at Serçe Limani in Turkish waters (see p.84–5).

Timber selection and conversion (see p.8–12)

Wherever available, oak (*Quercus sp.*) was used for the main elements of a Nordic ship; failing this, pine (*Pinus sp.*) and ash (*Fraxinus sp.*) were used. Specific shapes and lengths of timber were chosen to match each particular element: natural crooks for framing and for tholes; long, straight-grained, knot-free boles for planking. A first step was to remove the bark then the sapwood, yet, on almost every early vessel excavated, some sapwood has been found. To the advantage of twenty-first century dendro-chronologists, Nordic builders occasionally left sapwood on timbers so that they could be fashioned to a desired shape.

Pine logs were converted by splitting the log into two and working each half into a plank. Oak logs were split into two and then split radially into halves, then halves again, and again, so that, from a sound bole, sixteen planks ('clove boards') were obtained (Fig. 1.6). Keels, stems and framing timbers were fashioned by reducing a log or a half-log, following the natural run of the grain whenever possible.

Nordic shipbuilding presupposed a good supply of quality timber to provide high grade boards and crooks. From the eleventh century onwards, however, there seems to have been a shortage of large, sound oaks: planks were re-cycled and immature oaks felled so that shorter and narrower planks had to be used.

Axes were used to fell trees and to trim them. Logs were split using hardwood (sometimes hafted metal) wedges, driven by a mallet. Saws had been introduced to north-west Europe by the Romans, but they do not appear to have been used in northern shipyards until the thirteenth century. Planks were also fashioned by axe (Fig. 1.7) but planes were sometimes used to work bevels in the lap. Holes were bored by a spoon-shaped bit in an auger; profile or moulding irons were used to cut linear decorations; draw knives and adzes for the curved shapes needed in frames; chisels, shaves and slices for fine work; hammer, chisel, nail-heading iron and files for the numerous nails needed. Block and tackle, rollers, sheerlegs 'Spanish' windlasses, cramps, shores and spalls were also essential on the building site.

The Nordic ship of the 11th-12th century
A typical Nordic ship of this period may be described under three headings.

Form: A double-ended vessel with a smooth keel/post transition, a generally rounded bottom with flaring sides, and a distinctive sheerline leading to high ends. (Figs 1.11 & 3.28).

Structure: These vessels were essentially 'open boats', although cargo vessels had a short deck at each end. Ships and boats were built plank-first, the relatively thin planking being fashioned to give the required hull shape. The uppermost and waterline strakes were generally thicker than the others and, with the keel, were the main longitudinal strength members of the hull. Planks within strakes were joined together in a simple overlapping scarf; strakes were fastened together clinker

Fig. 3.28. 'Sea Stallion from Glendalough' – a reconstruction of the great warship, Skuldelev 2, under sail in the Baltic.

fashion, with nails clenched inboard by distorting the point over a rove (Fig.1.3D).

The keel, of T-shaped cross section, protruded below the hull and was joined to the stems in a vertical scarf fastened by clenched nails. Stems were either rabbetted to receive the planking ends, or they were hollowed in section (thereby allowing the plank ends to be clench-fastened) and stepped in profile (thus providing sufficient landing for each plank end to be securely fastened to the stem).

Evenly-spaced, symmetrically-placed floor timbers were fastened by treenails to the lower planking, but not to keel or garboards. Above every floor, there was a lower crossbeam supported by standing, and sometimes by lodging (horizontal), knees to the planking. A second level of beams and knees was fastened at every station in warships, and at selected stations in cargo ships in which there could also be a third level of beams. Pillars were fastened between floor and beam, and between lower and higher beams. Side timbers supported planking between frame stations in the upper hull which was further stiffened by sets of longitudinally-running stringers.

Propulsion and steering. Ships and large boats were propelled by a square sail on a mast stepped near amidships in a longitudinal keelson which fitted over, and was fastened to, several floors so that it rested on the keel but was not fastened to it. The mast beam, at a higher level, further supported the mast. Standing rigging included forestay and shrouds – braces do not seem to have been used but may have appeared towards the end of this period, as may reef points. Running rigging included a halyard, sheets and a parrel between yard and mast. The tacking spar (holding the luff of the square sail into the wind) was used from the eleventh century and may have been supplemented by a bowline.

Warships were also propelled by oar with two oarsmen to a bench. Small cargo ships could be propelled by two or three oarsmen at bow and stern; it seems unlikely that the larger cargo ships had this facility.

Steering was by side rudder held to the ship's starboard quarter at two points on its shaft so that it could be rotated about its own long axis by a thwartships tiller. Rudders protruded well below the level of the keel thereby offsetting some of the leeway created when sailing across wind. Some rudders could continue to be used in shoal waters after their upper shaft had been canted forward to bring the blade above keel level.

Nordic characteristics. A Nordic vessel was a built as a light, buoyant structure which gave it advantages in both roles: merchant ships could carry relatively more cargo; warships could be operated in shallow, coastal waters and taken up rivers. These vessels had 'sweet lines' which gave warships high speed potential under oars. The larger cargo ships were capable of ocean voyages: they did not need formal harbour

Fig. 3.29. The reconstruction of the early-11th century cargo ship, Skuldelev 1, heading towards Roskilde cathedral.

facilities but were loaded and unloaded after taking the ground or having anchored. In sea trials a reconstruction of the larger cargo ship, *Skuldelev 1* (Fig. 3.29), achieved 8.5 knots maximum, made ground to windward at 1.2- 1.5 knots, and could sail up to 68° (plus leeway) off the wind.

Later Nordic ships. Although Nordic ships continued to have an 'open-boat' appearance, they undertook ocean voyages to Greenland and beyond: this achievement reflects the hardiness and fortitude of the crew rather than the virtues of their ships. By the thirteenth century, however, Nordic cargo ships depicted on the town seals of Winchelsea, Sandwich and Yarmouth had crossbeams protruding through their sides at a level that suggests that such vessels had a near-full–length deck. Not only would that deck have strengthened the hull and increased the vessel's seaworthiness, but also it would have provided a sheltered space in which the crew could sleep and eat.

Ratios of seven excavated cargo vessels, from the late twelfth to the mid-fourteenth century, give a mean L/B of 3.3 (compared with 3.7 in earlier centuries) and L/D of 7.2 (compared with 8.8): thus the later ships and boats were deeper and broader. Moreover, on the thirteenth century Sandwich town seal the ship has a boat onboard which suggests that ships had become bigger. Ship's timbers re-used in Dublin, show that there was a significant increase in size of vessels using the port in the late twelfth to early thirteenth century. Furthermore, ships had relatively larger holds: the hold index increased from 0.28-0.34 in the eleventh century, to *c.*0.48 in the thirteenth.

There were other structural changes: superstructures known as 'castles' were built at bow and stern; a top was fitted near the mast head; and, as seen on the thirteenth century Sandwich seal, protruding crossbeams had fairings over their ends to prevent snagging when going alongside waterfronts or other vessels. Plank scarfs became longer and therefore stronger: in Dublin, for example, scarf gradients decreased from 21-33 % to 8-16%. A more fundamental change was the use of sawn (rather than split) planking, from the thirteenth century. By the late thirteenth/early fourteenth century ships were built from sawn planks that were generally 12ft or less in length.

From the early thirteenth century, yards were held to the mast by a composite parrel with trucks (balls) and ribs (laths). Reef points were depicted on the Dublin seal of 1297, and bonnets appeared in the fourteenth century enabling the mariner to vary sail area to match the wind. The ship on the 1300 Yarmouth seal seems to have a bowline from the luff of its sail to a bowsprit. Braces (used to trim the yard and thus the sail) are depicted on the thirteenth century Winchelsea seal (Fig. 3.30). In the fourteenth century top sails were added to the single square sail that had been used heretofore.

The side rudder continued to be fitted to the starboard quarter into the thirteenth century. Stern rudders on Nordic vessel are depicted on the thirteenth century seals of Poole and Ipswich; they had earlier appeared on hulcs depicted on late twelfth century fonts at Winchester and at Zedelgem in Belgium.

Fig. 3.30. The 13th century town seal of Winchelsea depicting a late development of the Nordic ship. (National Maritime Museum, Greenwich)

In the thirteenth century, Nordic shipbuilders seem to have responded to the challenge of the cog by reducing the cost of building and operating their cargo ships. Planking and framing techniques were simplified, ships were increased in size and holds made relative bigger; furthermore, techniques were borrowed from the cog: sawn planking, raked posts and suchlike. The Nordic ship became more utilitarian, rather than a 'delight to the eye'. By the fifteenth century the Nordic merchant ship was almost indistinguishable from the cog. The 1418 warship *Grace Dieu*, of Henry V of England, may have been the last large ship built in the Nordic manner, that is with overlapping planking fastened together by clenched nails. Subsequent large vessels, both merchant and warships, were built frame-first with non-edge-fastened planking. Nordic building techniques lived on, however, in the smaller craft of northern Europe particularly in Norway and Shetland, but also further afield in Ireland, Britain and northern America – even until today.

The Cog

The Anglo-Saxon Chronicle (Parker Ā) noted that in AD 897 King Alfred ordered warships to be built that were 'neither after the Frisian design, nor after the Danish'. In the sixth century AD Frisians, who were notable seamen, lived on the coast between the Elbe and Rhine deltas and on the chain of islands lying to the west and north, as far as Syldt. It has been suggested that their vessels were early forms of what became known as 'cogs'.

The type name 'cog' was first noted in ninth century documents referring to Frisian shipping and trade. In the thirteenth and fourteenth centuries there are many references to them, including their use by the Hanseatic League on coastal passage from the Rhine mouth to Scandinavia in the north, and to Gdansk Bay in the east; they were also used for trade between Britain and Ireland and the Continent. Crusaders and pilgrims from northern Europe were transported to the Mediterranean in cogs, and, in 1304, the Florentine chronicler, Villani, noted that from that time Genoese, Venetians and Catalonian shipyards began to build cogs which were both cheaper and more seaworthy than their own ships.

The link between documentary and iconographic evidence of the cog was established by Fliedner (1964) who realised that the fifteenth century citizens of Stralsund had called their fourteenth century town seal 'the cog'. The ship depicted on this 1329 seal (Fig.3.31) had clinker planking and a single mast stepped amidships (as did the Nordic ship) but was distinctive in having straight, raked bow and sternpost; moderate sheer towards bow and stern; a relatively deep hull; castles at bow and stern; and a centreline rudder. A large, almost complete, hull excavated in 1962 from the River Weser, downstream from Bremen, proved to have many of those features and was identified as a cog. Dendrochronology dated this ship to 1378: thus she is a late example of a cog.

Fig. 3.31. A cog depicted on the 1329 town seal of Stralsund.

A number of thirteenth to fifteenth century ships with similar characteristics have been excavated from Dutch, Danish, Swedish and

German waters, of which eighteen have been dendro-dated: two to the late twelfth century, four to the thirteenth, eleven to the fourteenth, and one to the early fifteenth. Of these, nine have been provenanced: three (oldest) to South Jutland; four, the Baltic; one, River Weser and one to the Netherlands.

As in all shipbuilding traditions, the vessels identified as cogs form a polythetic group: no one vessel has to have all characteristics and no single characteristic has to be held by all members of that group. Although not all excavated cogs have so far been published in detail, it is possible to identify a provisional group of characteristic that define the cog.

Form

Double-ended vessels with straight, raked posts, a flat bottom, longitudinally, with a sharp transition between bottom and posts. The cog sheerline rises gently at the stern, more so at the bow where the stempost protrudes above the planking. Transversely, cogs have a full form with rounded bilges and a slight deadrise of the garboards from the plank-keel. Seagoing cogs have flared upper sides, while the sides of river vessels are near-vertical. Of the cogs that have been hypothetically reconstructed, the mean $L/D = 9.4 \pm 2.9$ (contemporary Nordic vessels: 8.3 ± 1.7); $L/B = 3.37 \pm 0.58$ (compared with 3.30 ± 0.54).

Structure

Cogs had a plank-keel, approximately twice the thickness of their garboard strakes. A crook, shaped to give the ship a <u>skeg</u> forward and a heel aft, was scarfed to plank-keel and posts at each end of the ship. Over most of its length, the bottom planking was not fastened together or to the plank-keel, but laid edge-to-edge. Towards the ends, this planking was turned through 90° (probably after charring) by notching, sculpting and bevelling, so that it became overlapping; it was then nailed into rabbets in the lower stems and in the transition timber ('stem hook') between plank-keel and stems.

The side planking was also laid overlapping fastened together by nails clenched inboard by hooking. Caulking was done after fastening, using tarred moss and sometimes cattle hair. In the edge-to-edge bottom planking, this caulking was forced from outboard between the seams; a lath was then placed along each seam and held in place by butterfly-shaped iron clamps (<u>sintels</u>). The clinker side-planking was caulked by placing tarred moss in a cove cut (before the upper plank was fitted) near the upper, outboard edge of each strake, and held in place by lath and <u>sintels</u>. Planks within strakes were joined in a vertical scarf fastened by hooked nails with a moss caulking. Most cogs excavated have relatively thick, sawn planking; the Kollerup cog of AD 1150 (the oldest-known cog to date) had planking fashioned from half-logs.

Floor timbers, which were substantial when compared with those in Nordic vessels, were generally laid with extensions alternately to port and starboard and treenailed to the planking. Above them were futtocks and top timbers up to the sheer strake. Stringers and other timbers were fitted to reinforce the upper planking.

Crossbeams were fastened by hanging and standing knees to the planking of seagoing cogs: one became mast beam, one was at each end of the hold and the remainder were regularly spaced. Beams protruded through the cog's sides and their ends were protected by fairings, as seen, for example, on 1350 seal of Elbing. The Bremen cog has a fifth cross beam, at a higher level forward, to which bits were fastened to take the cable when the ship was riding at anchor. Large, deep knees stood on the beams of the Bremen cog and were treenailed to them and to the side planking. Removable deck planking was laid athwartships on carlings, fore-and-aft timbers that had been let into the upper face of the large knees and were themselves supported by smaller knees.

Although forecastles appear on some cog depictions, there is little, if any; excavated evidence for them. Aftercastles are generally depicted, and the Bremen cog has a well-integrated, raised superstructure aft, from which the ship would have been conned and sailed.

Propulsion and steering
Although small cogs used on inland waters probably had auxiliary

oars, seagoing cogs were propelled by sail alone. A single sail was set on a mast stepped some 30% to 40% of the ship's waterline length, from forward. Crumlin-Pedersen has pointed out that the earliest-known cog (Kollerup) had her mast-step well forward, before the hold, at 29% of her overall length (a similar position to the mast on seagoing ships of the Romano-Celtic tradition). Later cogs had masts stepped nearer midships: Kolding (AD 1189) at 34%; Vejby (1372) at 42% and Bremen (1380) at 43%. Dutch cogs for inland waters continued to have their masts stepped well forward, the optimum position for towing.

It may be that Kollerup and Kolding set a fore-and-aft sail (a lugsail?) but, from the early fourteenth century, cogs set a square sail. The cog depicted on the 1365 seal of Kiel has a sail that is canted, leading to the suggestion that masters of later cogs set a square sail in a way that gained some of the advantages of the fore-and aft sail. No sail or rigging has been excavated with a cog, but representational evidence shows standing rigging consisting of stays and shrouds. The Bremen cog had a windlass aft for hoisting yard and sail, and a capstan at a higher level forward, for working sheets

The Kollerup cog (without a keelson) had her mast step in a floor timber (as in the seagoing vessels of the Romano-Celtic tradition). Apart from two Dutch river cogs, other cogs had a keelson that was treenailed to the floors but not to the plank-keel. When compared with the length of their associated plank-keel, keelson lengths ranged from 50% (Kolding of 1189), to 80% (Vejby of 1372) and 72% (Bremen of 1380).

Building sequence
In two cog wrecks, small, square holes, plugged with treenails, have been found throughout the bottom planking, and in some of the clenched side planking. It has been concluded that these were where battens had been fastened to hold the bottom planking firmly together before floors were fitted. No such evidence was found on the Bremen cog, but square holes have been noted on the wreck from Vejby. The builders of the Hamburg reconstruction of the Bremen cog used

battens; those building the Kiel reconstruction used temporary lashings.

The building sequences published for the Bremen, the Almere and NZ43 cogs are similar and may be summarised:

- stem hooks scarfed to plank-keel, and main posts to stem hooks;
- bottom planking fashioned, fitted and fastened together at the ends in an overlap, their central sections temporarily fastened together with lashings or battens;
- floors fashioned, fitted and fastened to bottom planking, keelson fastened to floors, lashings/battens removed, bottom caulked externally;
- first five side strakes fashioned, fastened together overlapping and to hooks and posts, and caulked inboard;
- main crossbeams inserted and supported by knees; possibly some futtocks added;
- after two more strakes, higher crossbeams and all remaining futtocks inserted;
- two more strakes and washstrakes added, then the top timbers.
- great knees / half bulkheads added;
- ceiling planking, longitudinal timbers and decking added – then superstructure.

<u>Cog performance</u>

It has been estimated that the seagoing Kollerup cog could have carried *c*.30 tonnes; two river vessels, 24.5 tonnes (Almere) and 9 tonnes (NZ43); and the Bremen cog between 70 and 130 tonnes. Trials of the Kiel-built reconstruction of the Bremen cog indicated that her maximum useful cargo capacity was 87 tonnes at a draft of 2.25m. Sailing trials in the Baltic showed that this 'floating hypothesis' could sail for a short while as close as 75° to the true wind, making *c*.1 knot to windward. Generally, however, the best she could achieve was a track 90° off the wind. She performed best on a broad reach and when running, achieving eight knots. In any sort of seaway, however, she developed a jerky motion which led 'to considerable strain on the crew'. Moreover, her performance was limited by not having a watertight weather deck. The general conclusion was that this hypothetical reconstruction of the Bremen cog was not a windward vessel. Although her hull is probably authentic, having been derived from excavated remains, her rig had to be based on seal depictions and theoretical calculations which may have led to poor sailing capabilities.

The feature that medieval ship builders evidently aimed to maximise in the cog was her cargo carrying capacity. A box-shaped hold was combined with an underwater shape that allowed the ship to take the ground in tidal conditions and sit upright, yet with sufficiently fine ends to give a reasonable performance under sail. Cogs probably had a stiffer and stronger hull than Nordic ships, and size for size, were heavier since their framing scantlings were greater. In this respect the cog may be seen as a member of the same heavy structural approach to shipbuilding as the Romano-Celtic tradition some 1,000 years earlier. The stress per unit area in Romano-Celtic ships and in the Cog tradition was less than in the Nordic light tradition which required high quality trees with knot-free, straight-grained boles with crooks in the crown. Rather than having to seek such a limited (therefore expensive) stock, cogs could be built from oaks widely available. Furthermore, the cog could be built from sawn rather than split timber.

The cog and the Romano-Celtic tradition

It is generally considered that the cog style of shipbuilding originated in Frisian lands in and near the mouth of the Rhine. Much of the evidence for the riverine boats of the first to fourth centuries AD. Romano-Celtic tradition also comes from that region: the three seagoing vessels of that tradition, on the other hand, were excavated off the island of Guernsey, in the River Thames at London and in a river flowing into the Severn Estuary in south-west Wales.

There were two versions in each of these traditions: flat-bottomed hulls for river and canal boats; rounded hulls of full form with a protruding plank–keel for seagoing vessels. A principal difference between the two traditions is that Romano-Celtic seagoing ships were built framing–first; the cog, an unusual form of plank-first. Both versions of both traditions were built from sawn planking and their framing was in the 'heavy' tradition. Both were double-ended and had a plank-keel to which was fastened, in the Romano-Celtic vessels, a curved, L-shaped stem, and, in the cog tradition, a stem hook and a raked post. In both traditions the bottom planking was not fastened together (except in the ends of cogs) or to the plank-keel. Hooked nails were used in both traditions: in the cog, overlapping planking was fastened together by iron nails clenched inboard by hooking; builders of Romano-Celtic ships had used similarly-clenched nails to fasten flush-laid planking to framing.

Early sea-going cogs were similar to Romano-Celtic sea-going vessels in having mast-steps well forward in a heavy framing timber rather than in a longitudinal keelson. Moreover, in the early stages of building some of the inland Romano-Celtic boats (type A), hull planking was temporarily held together with ropes, or battens were nailed to them, until floor timbers could be inserted. This technique became a key aspect in cog building and was subsequently used in sixteenth to seventeenth century, seagoing Dutch ships in the Rhine mouth region – a feature sometimes called 'Double-Dutch'. Ole Crumlin-Pedersen pointed out, more than thirty years ago, that such similarities strongly suggest that early Hanseatic cogs were built using techniques that, a thousand years earlier, had been used by the builders of Romano-Celtic ships and boats.

Hulcs

Vessels thought to be *hulcs* are depicted on early ninth-century coins issued by Charlemagne, by Louis the Pious and by Athelstan the First of East Anglia. These vessels are double-ended, single- masted ships with a curved longitudinal profile, with their planking ending, not on stems, but on a near-horizontal plane above the waterline. The first documentary reference to the '*hulc*' is in the *c.*AD 1000 laws of Aethelred the Second of England: tolls of equal value were to be paid by *hulcs* and by *ceol*/keels (probably Nordic ships) when they discharged cargo at Billingsgate on the River Thames in London. In

AD 1130 regulations, concerning the import of Rhenish wine, it was stated that keels should pay a greater toll than *hulcs*; by the fourteenth century *hulcs* payed more than keels. From this, it appears that, whereas in the period from AD 1000 to the mid-twelfth century *hulcs* carried much the same amount of cargo as keels, by the fourteenth century, they carried a greater load. Thirteenth to fifteenth century documents show that, in *c*.AD 1400, Hanseatic merchants began to use *hulcs* in the Baltic and, by the mid-fifteenth century *hulcs* had entirely replaced cogs there.

The link between these references to *hulcs* and representations of them was made in 1956 by Heinsius who recognised that the Latin inscription on the 1295 civic seal of New Shoreham (Fig. 3.32) in Sussex, in translation, read: 'By this symbol of a hulc I am called mouth which is a worthy name'. Documents of the fourteenth and fifteenth centuries in the West Sussex Record Office refer to 'Hulkesmouth alias Shoreham'. The seal shows that the late thirteenth century *hulc* was double-ended with castles at bow and stern, but without visible stems and keel. Her planking appears to be laid in reverse-clinker – each strake overlaps inboard the upper edge of the strake below, rather than overlapping outboard as in Nordic clinker. The *hulc*'s planking runs in a curve parallel to the sheerline and to the bottom of the hull, and ends, not at stems, but on a horizontal line at the base of each castle, well above the waterline. Such planking patterns are suitable for a beamy, full-ended and capacious hull. The depicted ship has a single mast stepped near amidships, a rudder on the starboard quarter and an anchor catted in the bows: similar features appear on other representations, including the late twelfth century font in Winchester Cathedral.

As reverse-clinker is otherwise unknown in European waters, it might be thought that those depictions of reverse clinker are an 'artist's mistake'. However, reverse-clinker is used widely in Bangladesh and in the Indian east coast states of Orissa and West Bengal: there is now a wealth of information about twentieth century South Asian boats with *hulc* planking runs, with or without reverse-clinker planking. In the absence of excavated evidence for a *hulc*, the present, medieval depictions of reverse-clinker have to be taken at face value. If and when parts of a European *hulc* are excavated, that ethnographic evidence may prove invaluable in their interpretation.

LATE-MEDIEVAL SHIPS

From the late thirteenth century, interaction between Mediterranean and North-west European seamen and shipbuilders increased, resulting in the transfer of shipbuilding techniques in both directions. By this time Mediterranean ships had been built framing-first for more than 600 years. Frame-first

Fig. 3.32. A hulc cargo ship depicted on the 1295 town seal of New Shoreham in Sussex.

building had also been practised in the Celtic lands of north-west Europe from the second century AD until the fourth/fifth (see p.131). The fact that the cog, originating in the Rhine mouth region, was built plank-first, apart from its bottom, suggests that, by that time, the framing-first sequence was no longer used in those lands settled by Germanic people in the fifth century.

Framing-first may, however, have survived in Ireland. Dr Michael McCaughan has noted that an indigenous tradition of frame-first plank-boat building has survived on the remote and culturally-retentive western seaboard of Ireland. This is a separate, and much older, tradition than the nineteenth century AD, frame-first building that was introduced on Ireland's relatively innovative, east coast where, until then, plank-first, clinker-built boats had predominated. McCaughan has suggested that this west coast, frame-first technique was not younger, but older than the plank-first techniques that had been brought to Ireland by Vikings. It may be that, as in southern Britain, frame-first was used to build plank boats in Ireland in the early centuries AD.

Frame-first caravels were built in northern Europe from the mid-fifteenth century onwards and frame-first shipbuilding gradually ousted plank-first over much of Atlantic Europe. The earliest references to design methods needed in frame-first building, are from Venice. By the sixteenth century similar methods were used in Italy, Iberia, France, the southern Netherlands and England. Seven early sixteenth century wrecks, five of which may have been built in the Iberian peninsula, were probably designed and built framing-first: in this respect, they were similar to Romano-Celtic vessels. The formal design methods described in Venetian texts were probably preceded by informal methods using measurement units and ratios. Vestiges of those Venetian/Iberian methods (sometimes known as 'Mediterranean moulding') have recently been found to be used in Newfoundland, Brazil and Tamil Nadu. The post-medieval adoption of frame-first techniques in Atlantic Europe meant that stronger, more seaworthy ships were built. It also meant that a design that proved itself at sea could be repeated again and again.

ATLANTIC SEAFARING

From at least Neolithic times, boats were used by north-west European seamen in coastal waters and to cross channels such as that between France and England. Subsequently, Phoenicians and Greeks sailed the southern coast of Spain and, in the fourth century BC, Pytheas sailed, probably in a series of short-haul passages, from the Pillars of Hercules (or possibly the River Garonne) to the estuary of the Rhine and beyond. In Roman times, although vessels continued to sail along the Iberian Atlantic coast to and from the Bay of Biscay, much trade between the Mediterranean and north-west Europe went by French and German rivers, the final leg being by sea along the Atlantic coast from the estuaries of the Garonne, Loire, Seine and Rhine. Vikings sailed the Atlantic coast into the Mediterranean in the ninth century and, in the tenth century, Arabs ventured northwards along that coast. Chaucer's fourteenth century shipman knew the 'harbours and havens of the coast from Gotland to Cape Finisterre, and the creeks of Brittany and Spain'. Moreover, he knew his tides, streams, the phases of the moon, and tracks and distances: Neolithic seamen probably had similar knowledge.

During the Medieval period navigational instruments began to be used: the magnetic compass, from the late twelfth century; the sand glass, traverse tables, astrolabes, quadrants, sailing directions and charts, from the fifteenth century. Nevertheless, vessels sailing the Atlantic coast did so from the vicinity of one known landmark to another – a process known as 'cape-ing the ship'. In the early fifteenth century Iberian and Genoese seamen re-discovered the Canary Islands and discovered the Madeiras and the Azores, the latter some 800 nautical miles out into the Atlantic. The long route to India was pioneered by Dias in 1488 and by Vasco da Gama in 1497-9. Thus by 1492, Columbus was heir to a wealth of navigational practices. Nevertheless, although he used a chart and magnetic compass, he did not use the astrolabe and quadrant that he had onboard *Santa Maria*: he preferred 'dead reckoning', the simplest form of navigation: time measured by sand-glass and by the relative positions of the two 'guards' in Ursa Minor; speeds and distances estimated. Without chart, compass or sand-glass, tenth century Viking seamen had used similar non-instrumental methods to cross the north Atlantic. Indeed, comparable methods had been used worldwide from the earliest days of seafaring.

CHAPTER 4

In Conclusion

The chapters of this book are as comprehensive as the author has been able to make them, yet, when considered objectively, they are remarkably sketchy with enormous temporal and spatial gaps. For example, no water transport dated earlier than 7,000 BC is mentioned since none has yet been excavated, although it is clear that, by that date, Man, the boatbuilder and seaman, had been active for millennia. Moreover, there are no excavated examples of the four types of float; only one example (the log raft) has been excavated, of four types of raft, and only three types (log, plank and bundle) of the six forms of boat.

As excavation techniques are developed, it seems possible that the date of 7,000 BC for the earliest known boat remains will be pushed back. For floats and rafts, however, this may prove impossible because of their near-ephemeral nature and the fact that their constituent parts could have been readily re-used for other purposes when they were no longer sea-worthy. Hide boats and bundle boats also rapidly degrade when abandoned, leaving a biased sample of water transport to be excavated.

There may also be bias in our knowledge of plank boat and logboats. In Atlantic Europe, (excluding northern Scandinavia) the overwhelming majority of excavated boats are found to be of oak (*Quercus sp*), a species which has a relatively high durability and is therefore more likely to survive than most other species. There are reasons for believing that this preponderance of oak reflects its usage in ancient boatbuilding, nevertheless, bias may have occurred and that possibility has to be borne in mind.

BOATBUILDING TRADITIONS
Sewn plank boats
After a century or so of excavation and research in Europe and in European waters, it has proved possible to identify a number of planked-boat building traditions, within each one of which vessels share many features: 'Classical' and 'Byzantine' in the Mediterranean; 'Romano-Celtic', 'Nordic' and 'Cog' in Atlantic Europe. Sewn plank boats excavated in the Mediterranean and in Atlantic Europe (as well as in Egypt and in South-east Asia) have proved difficult to classify, although one distinguishing trait appears to be in the type of plank fastening: boats with individual lashings as plank fastenings are earlier than boats with continuous sewing.

Romano-Celtic seagoing vessels
Compared with the numerous, excavated ships and boats of the Mediterranean 'Classical' tradition and the Atlantic Europe 'Nordic' tradition, the number of Romano-Celtic seagoing boats and ships is minute. The three (possibly four) second to fourth century AD vessels are, at present, the earliest known in the world to have been built 'framing-first'. To confirm this group's characteristic features and to investigate their relationship to the contemporary 'Rhine barges' (which share some of their features) we need to investigate more examples of Romano-Celtic seagoing boat. Moreover, the link (if any) between these craft and those of the tenth to fifteenth century AD Cog tradition, remains to be investigated, as does the relationship of Romano-Celtic vessels and the Cog to the fifteenth to sixteenth century framing-first vessels of Atlantic Europe: the latter were the first European ships to undertake oceanic voyages and thus open the world to European eyes and to trade. Should an example of the 'mysterious hulc' turn up during this research, maritime archaeologists would indeed become overwhelmed with 'riches'.

EXPERIMENTAL ARCHAEOLOGY
When measured against the amount of publicity given to it, during the past thirty years, experimental boat archaeology has contributed

remarkably little to our knowledge of the past. In the main, this has been because most experimental projects have been undertaken in a less-than-scientific manner: conclusions drawn were not securely based on demonstrable evidence. Moreover, in almost every such project, the focus of effort has been on the building and (especially) the sea trials of such vessels rather than on the theoretical transformation of the excavated remains – disturbed, fragmented and incomplete – into a valid, scale model of the original vessel's form, structure, propulsion and steering. Furthermore, such models should undergo specialist criticism well before the building of a full-scale vessel is considered.

To date, valid ship archaeological experiments are pitifully few: possibly only the Danish experiment to reconstruct, build and sail 'replicas' of the five Skuldelev wrecks excavated from Roskilde fjord; and the Anglo-American-Greek project that used reverse-engineering techniques to design, build and sail a 'floating hypothesis' of a fifth century BC Athenian trireme. Both these experiments seem to have resulted in reconstructions that are as close as it is now possible to get to the original prototype. Future experimenters would do well to learn from these projects and, before seeking grants and raw materials, ensure that their aims, and their intended method of achieving those aims, are based on rigorous arguments. Hypothetical reconstruction of the original form and structure of the excavated remains of a vessel is not yet an exact science. It is highly desirable that the highest standards are maintained so that public confidence in such activities is not irretrievably lost.

THE IDENTIFICATION OF A WRECK'S 'HOME PORT'

Rafts, boats and ships travel and may be wrecked, and thus enter the archaeological record, far from their place of origin. For example, medieval wrecks have been excavated from Chinese waters and from within the south-east Asian archipelago that appear to have been involved in trade between those two maritime regions. Although certain features of individual vessels seems to identify their region of origin (south-east Asia or China), further excavations are desirable, and more research is essential, so that this distinction may be verified.

That boats are mobile (under their own propulsion or involuntarily) has also been overlooked in two European prehistoric boat projects (Ch. 3) in which it appears to have been assumed that where a boat is excavated is necessarily where she had spent her working life. A boat fragment recovered from the foreshore at Kilnsea on the Yorkshire coast, north of the Humber estuary, was not necessarily from a boat based there: it seems intrinsically more likely that a fragment from a boat that had been disabled within the Humber estuary (her regular operational area) was swept out of that estuary and deposited on the east coast. An alternative explanation is also possible for the prehistoric boat remains excavated from a former river bed in Dover. That boat could well have been a ferry (as were her near-contemporaries in the Humber and Severn estuaries) from and to Sheppey, an island that, until the fourteenth century AD, lay off the coast of north-east Kent. After a mishap, that boat may well have drifted southwards to eventually be deposited in the tidal river at Dover.

In the interpretation of excavated wreck sites, it is essential to consider all logical possibilities: a most likely explanation may then arise, if there proves to be overwhelming evidence for it, otherwise, it may be necessary to decide that there is no way of choosing between several possibilities.

INTERNATIONAL CO-OPERATION

In addition to widely-based efforts to increase the rigour with which experimental boat archaeological projects are tackled, international co-operation is needed to facilitate the compilation and publication of a dictionary of nautical and technical terms used in maritime archaeology, and to encourage funding bodies to support research into early coastal environments with the ultimate aim of drawing reliable maps/charts of the European Atlantic coastline and estuaries, at intervals back to Neolithic times, or even earlier. When such maps/charts are available archaeologists will be better placed to understand the problems faced by early seamen working in coastal waters and estuaries.

It is not clear what body could oversee such a programme of research. The international body, ISBSA, founded almost forty years ago at the National Maritime Museum, Greenwich, has not taken up a suggestion made to them some twenty-five years ago, that they should assume that role. Moreover, both the Nautical Archaeology Society and the Society for Nautical Research appear not to be interested: the former body evidently concentrating mainly on underwater excavation; and the latter focused on the historical period centred on Admiral Nelson's lifetime. It may be that a new group will have to be formed, if research-based maritime archaeology ('the study of the nature and the past behaviour of Man in his use of those special environments associated with lakes, rivers and seas') is to become effective internationally.

Further Reading

General

Anon., 2001. *Dictionary of the World's Watercraft*. Mariners' Museum: Newport News. and London: Chatham Publishing

Delgado, J. (ed), 1997. *Encyclopaedia of Underwater & Maritime Archaeology*. London: British Museum Press.

Greenhill, B. 1995. *Archaeology of Boats and Ships*. Conway Maritime Press.

Hornell, J. 1946. *Water Transport*. Cambridge: Cambridge University Press. repr. 1970, Newton Abbot: David & Charles.

McGrail, S. 2004. *Boats of the World*. 2nd (paperback) edition. Oxford : Oxford University Press.

International Journal of Nautical Archaeology. Journal of the Nautical Archaeology Society – obtainable from: N.A.S. Fort Cumberland. Portsmouth. PO4 9LD.

Note: Greek and Roman authors, writing between 700 BC and AD 100, illuminate aspects of their maritime world: Homer; Herodotus; Julius Caesar; Vitruvius; Strabo; and Pliny. See references to these authors (and to the Bible) within the text.

Ch 1. Concepts & Techniques

Anderson, A. Barrett, J.H. & Boyle, K.V. 2010. *Global Origins & Development of Seafaring*. Cambridge: McDonald Institute Monograph.

Marchaj, C.A. 1964. *Sailing Theory & Practice* London: Adlard Coles.

McGrail, S. 1998. *Ancient Boats in North-West Europe*. 2nd ed. London: Longman.

Rawson K.J. & Tupper, E.C. 1976-7. *Basic Ship Theory*. 2 vols. Longman.

Steffy, J.R. 1994. *Wooden Shipbuilding and the Interpretation of Shipwrecks.* College Station: Texas A. & M. University Press.
Taylor, E.G.R. 1971. *Haven-Finding Art.* London: Hollis & Carter.
Ch. 2. Mediterranean
Basch, L. 1987. *Le musée imaginaire de la marine antique.* Athens: Inst. Hellénique pour la Préservation de la tradition nautique.
Casson, L. 1971. *Ships and Seamanship in the Ancient World.* Repr. with corrections 1996. Princeton: Princeton University Press.
Casson, L. 1989 *Periplus Maris Erythraei.* Princeton: Princeton University Press.
Kahanov, Y. & Linder, E. 2004. *Ma'agan Mikhael Ship.* Vol.2. Haifa: University of Haifa.
Linder, E. & Kahanov, Y. 2003. *Ma'agan Mikhael Ship* Vol. 1. Haifa: University of Haifa.
Morrison, J.S. Coates, J.F. & Rankov, N.B. 2000. *Athenian Trireme.* 2nd. ed. Cambridge: Cambridge University Press.
Parker, A.J. 1992. *Ancient Shipwrecks of the Mediterranean.* Oxford: BAR. S. 580.
Rankov, B. (ed) 2012. *Trireme Olympias.* Oxford: Oxbow Books
Rieth, E. 1996. *Le Maitre-Gabarit, La Tablette et Le Trébuchet.* Paris: CTHS.
Steffy, J.R. 1985. 'Kyrenia ship' *American J. of Archaeology,* 89: 71-101.
Steffy, J.R. 1994. *Wooden Shipbuilding & the Interpretation of Shipwrecks.* College Station: Texas A & M. University Press.
Wachsmann, S.1998. Seagoing *Ships & Seamanship in the Bronze Age Levant.* College Station: Texas A & M University Press.

Ch. 3 Atlantic Europe
Alves, F. (ed). 2001. *Proceedings of the International Symposium on the Archaeology of Medieval and Modern ships of the Iberian-Atlantic Tradition.*Lisbon: Inst.Português de Arqueologia.
Bately, J. & Englert, A.(ed) 2007 *Ohthere's Voyages.* Roskilde: Viking Ship Museum

Englert A. & Trakadas, A. (ed) 2009. *Wulfstan's Voyage.* Roskilde: Viking Ship Museum.

Binns, A.L. 1980. *Viking Voyagers.* London: Heinemann

Christensen, A-E. (ed) 1996. *History of the Ship: Earliest ships.* London: Conway Maritime Press.

Clark, P. (ed). 2004. *Dover Bronze Age Boat.* Swindon: English Heritage.

Cunliffe, B. 2001. *Facing the Ocean.* Oxford: Oxford University Press.

Crumlin-Pedersen, O. 1997. *Viking Age Ships & Shipbuilding in Hedeby & Schleswig.* Roskilde: Viking Ship Museum.

Crumlin-Pedersen, O. & Olsen, O. 2002. (ed). 'Skuldelev Ships 1'. *Ships & Boats of the North,* 4.1. Roskilde: Viking Ship Museum.

Flatman, J. 2009. *Ships & Shipping in Medieval Manuscripts.* London: British Library.

Friel, I. 1995. *Good Ship.* London: British Museum Press.

McGrail, S. 1998. *Ancient Boats in NW Europe.* 2nd edition. London: Longman.

Marsden, P. 1994. *Ships of the Port of London.* Vol.1. London: English Heritage.

Mowat, R.J.C. 1996. *Logboats of Scotland.* Oxford: Oxbow.

Wright, E.V. 1990. *Ferriby Boats.* London: Routledge.

Glossary

Note: Several technical terms are discussed and illustrated in Chapter 1

altitude: angular height of a celestial body
aspect ratio (of a sail): height²/area
azimuth: horizontal, angular distance of a star from the north or south point of a <u>meridian</u>
batten: light strip of wood, similar to a <u>lath</u>
beam: the beam of a vessel is her broadest breadth, usually at the waterline
beam-tie: transverse strengthening member near the ends of a logboat
beating-spar: spar used to keep taut the weather edge of a square sail
belay: to make fast ('turn up') a line around a <u>cleat</u> or similar fitting
bevel: surface that has been angled to make it fit with another
bilge: region between sides and bottom of a boat
bipod: mast with two legs
bireme: oared vessel with two levels of oarsmen
bitts: stout vertical posts to which lines and cables can be <u>belayed</u>
bole: main stem or trunk of a tree
bonnet: piece fastened to the foot of a sail to gain extra wind
boom: spar to which the foot of a sail is bent. See also <u>loose-footed</u>
bottom boards: lengths of timber fastened together and laid over the bottom of a boat as a flooring
bowline: a line to the bows from the luff (leading edge) of a square sail to keep the weather edge of the sail taut when a vessel is <u>close hauled</u>. See also <u>tacking spar</u> and <u>beating spar</u>
braces: lines to the yard arms – used to trim the <u>yard</u>
brail: rope used to bundle a sail, thereby reducing its effective area
bulkhead: transverse partition dividing a vessel into compartments

buoyancy: ability to float

capstan: revolving barrel rotated about a vertical axis by long bars set within holes around its head; used to work cables and weigh anchor

carlings: fore-and-aft timbers between crossbeams

catted: an anchor is catted, rather than hoisted to the hawse pipe, when it is brought to a special timber (the cat head) where it hangs clear of the bow

caulk: to insert material between two members thereby making the junction watertight

causeway: a raised way across a stretch of water or other wet place

ceiling: lining of planking over <u>floor timbers</u> and usually fastened to them

celestial pole: that point in the imaginary sphere in which the heavenly bodies lie about which that sphere appears to rotate

clamp: device for holding elements of a boat together (temporarily)

cleat: projection to which other fittings or a line are fastened

cleat rail: longitudinal <u>timber</u> incorporating several cleats

clench: deform, <u>hook</u> or <u>turn</u> the end of a nail fastening so that it will not draw out, may be done over a <u>rove</u>

clinker-built: a form of boatbuilding in which the <u>strakes</u> are placed so that they partly overlap one another- usually upper strake outboard of lower but, in South Asia, upper strake inboard of lower (<u>reverse-clinker</u>)

close-hauled: sailing as close to the wind as is possible

coiled-basketry: method of linking together reeds in which individual bundles are not only themselves bound but also interlinked with other bundles

cotter: a wooden pin that passes through a hole as a fastening

couple: pair of equal and parallel forces, acting in opposite directions and tending to cause rotation

cramp: wooden fitting drawing together two timbers across a seam

crook: curved piece of wood with the grain running along its length

crossbeam: <u>timber</u> extending across a vessel

day's sail: the distance an 'average' ship, in the 'usual' conditions, could be expected to sail in 24 hours. Distances between ports were said to be 'X days' sail'

deadrise: angle at which the bottom planking lies to the horizontal

deadweight: the carrying capacity of a ship expressed in tonnes weight

dendrology: the branch of science that deals with trees, especially the use of tree rings to deduce aspects of earlier climates

departure (to take): the last position of a ship, before losing sight of land, fixed from visual observation of landmarks

displacement: the weight (tonnage) of water a ship displaces when afloat, at certain loaded states

double-banked: said of oared boats when each oar is manned by two oarsmen

double-ended: a vessel that is (nearly) symmetrical about the midships transverse plane.

dowel: piece of wood, rounded in cross section, used to secure a loose tenon or to join together two other wooden pieces

draft: vertical distance between the waterline and the lowest point of a hull

drift: a movement downwind caused by the wind acting on sail and hull

dunnage: material, often wooden blocks, used to secure cargo in ships' holds

Dutchman's log: said to be used when speed is estimated by the time taken for a wood chip, dropped into the sea from the bow, to travel between two marks cut into the ship's gunwale

expanded (said of a logboat): after heat treatment (by sun, hot water or steam), the sides of a hollowed log are forced apart in a controlled manner, so that the breadth of the log near amidships increases, its midships height of sides decreases and its ends rise

extended (said of a logboat): washstrakes are fastened to each side of a hollowed log so that the height of side is increased; this can compensate for the decrease in side height of a logboat that has been expanded. Rarely, logboats may be extended in length.

fetch: distance of open water to windward of a stretch of coast

flare: transverse section of a boat increases in breadth towards the sheer

floor timber: transverse member, often a <u>crook</u>, set against the bottom planking from turn of <u>bilge</u> to turn of bilge; may be abbreviated to 'floor' (see <u>frame</u>)

flush-laid: <u>planking</u> in which adjoining <u>strakes</u> are butted edge-to-edge. To be distinguished from <u>clinker</u> planking in which one strake partly overlaps the other

fore-and-aft sail: sail generally set in or near the fore-and-aft line of a vessel

forefoot: junction of stem and keel

frame: transverse member set against the <u>planking</u> and made up of several <u>timbers</u>, usually a <u>floor</u> timber and a pair of <u>futtocks</u>

frame-first (skeleton–built): form of boatbuilding in which the framework of <u>keel</u>, posts and <u>frames</u> is set up and fastened together before the <u>planking</u> is fashioned

framing-first: form of boatbuilding in which <u>keel</u>, posts and elements of the lower framing are set up and fastened together before lower planking is fashioned and fastened to it; followed by more (higher) framing, then more planking

freeboard: height of sides above waterline

futtocks: elements of a <u>frame</u> that support the side planking; in a <u>frame-first</u> boat they define the shape of the lower hull. See: <u>side timber</u>

galley: vessel fitted for propulsion by oars and by sail

garboard: <u>strake</u> next to the <u>keel</u>; the lowest side strake

girdle: add additional planking at the waterline thereby increasing the vessel's breadth and thus improving transverse stability; also known as 'furring'

grapnel: a small anchor, for a boat rather than a ship

grommet: strands of rope layed up in the form of a ring

guares: retractable, wooden foil used to combat leeway and to alter course; a variable lee- board

gudgeon: an eyebolt on the sternpost, to receive the <u>pintle</u> of a rudder

GLOSSARY

halyard: line to hoist and lower yard and sail

hanging knee: a vertical knee below the structural member supported

hatchway: access via a hatch through the decks of a vessel

hog: the bending or shearing of a hull in the vertical plane, causing it to arch upwards in the middle and to drop at the ends

hogging hawser or stay: tensioned rope rigged on the centreline, high in the hull, to prevent hogging

hold: a space within a hull for the stowage of cargo

hooked nail: fastening nail that is clenched by turning its tip through 180°, back into the timber

hove-to: underway, but not making way through the water

interference fit: said of a treenail in a hole, or of a tenon in its mortise, when the wood fibres interlock

joggle: to cut a notch in a timber so that it will fit close against another member

keel: main longitudinal strength member, joined to the fore-stem forward and the after-stem or sternpost aft

keelson: centre-line timber above the floors, adding longitudinal strength and stiffness; may have a mast-step incorporated

knee: naturally-grown crook used as a bracket between two members at about right-angles to each other. See: 'hanging knee', 'lodging knee' and 'standing knee'

knot: one knot = one nautical mile per hour

land breeze: an evening/night wind that blows from land to sea when the land temperature falls below that of the sea

landfall: in open seas, to sight and identify a point of land

lath: light, longitudinal batten placed over caulking to protect it, and held in place by fastenings.

lateen: triangular, fore-and-aft sail bent to a long yard

leech: the sides of a square sail, one being the weather leech, the other, the lee leech; In fore-and-aft rig the leech is the trailing edge of the sail

leeboard: wooden board suspended over a boat's side to reduce leeway

lee platform: term used to describe a feature of certain Oceanic sailing craft; used as a balance board from which to trim the craft

lee shore: shore towards which predominant wind blows

leeway: angular difference between a sailing vessel's fore-and-aft line and the direction actually made good; drift downwind

lift: line running from yard arm to masthead

limber hole: notch cut in underside of frames to allow free circulation of bilge water

lines: (of a boat) interrelation of sections in different planes which show the shape of a boat's hull; usually consist of sheer plan, half-breadth plan and body plan

lodging knee: a horizontal knee

lofting floor: a room or gallery with a large area of floor on which the full-scale lines of a vessel can be drawn

loll: the state of a ship which is unstable when upright and therefore floats at an angle of heel, to one side or the other

loom: that part of an oar inboard of pivot

loose-footed: a sail without a boom at its foot

luff: leading edge of a fore-and-aft sail

lug: quadrilateral, fore-and-aft sail slung to leeward of the mast

mast step: fitting used to locate the heel of a mast; may be in keelson or floor timber

meridian: 'line of longitude': a semi-great circle, crossing the equator and parallels of latitude at right angles, and joining the earth's poles.

metacentre: theoretical point (M) in the middle plane of a vessel through which the buoyancy force passes when the vessel is inclined at a small angle

metacentric height: distance from the metacentre (M) to the centre of mass (G) of a loaded boat; a measure of a vessel's inherent stability

mizzen: the aftermost mast of a three-masted vessel

mortise and tenon: a method of fastening flush-laid planking in which free tenons are fitted into mortises cut in the edges of adjacent planks; after assembly, tenons may be pierced (locked) by two treenails, one in each plank. Formerly known as a 'draw-tongue joint'

moulded: dimension of a timber measured at right angles to the sided dimension

moulds: transverse wooden patterns giving the internal shape of a vessel

nautical mile: 1/60th of a degree on the equator: approx. 2,000 yards. 1 nautical mile approximately equals 10 Roman stades

oculus: an eyelike design on each bow; the ship's 'eyes'

outrigger: a counterpoising float rigged out from the side of a vessel to provide additional stability; some vessels have one on each side, others have a single outrigger which is mostly, but not always, kept to windward

paired boat: a boat with two hulls, side by side, sometimes known as 'double-hull'

parrel: a crook that holds a yard to the mast, yet allows the yard to pivot and to slide up and down. See trux and ribs

passage: a single journey at sea by a vessel, either outward or homeward.

pay: to cover a plank seam with hot pitch or coat a ship's bottom with a waterproofing substance

peak: upper, after corner of a four-sided, fore-and-aft sail

petroglyphs: rock art, graphic markings on a rock surface made for religious or other reasons. Sometimes known as 'pictographs'

pintle: metal pin on the leading edge of a rudder, by which the rudder hangs from the sternpost

plank: component of a strake that is not all in one piece

plank-first (shell-built): a form of boatbuilding in which the planking is (partly) erected and fastened together before framing is inserted

plank-keel: a keel-like timber of which the ratio of its moulded dimension to its sided dimension is ≤ 0.70

rabbet: groove or channel worked in a member to accept another, without a lip being formed

raked: angled away from the vertical; also degree of overhang of a vessel's ends

rays: layers of parenchyma cells in horizontal strands running out from the centre of a tree towards the circumference

reach: to sail with the wind from slightly forward of abeam to slightly aft

reef: shorten sail by tying up the lower portion using reef points

reconstruction: see Ch. 1: Research Sequence – interpretation

reverse-clinker: a form of boatbuilding in which strakes are laid so that they partly overlap each other, higher strake inboard of lower

rib: a simple form of frame; also laths in a parrel that keep the trux separate

ribband: a flexible strip of wood, heavier than a batten, temporarily fastened to framing to assess fairness, and to establish the run of the planking

rocker: fore-and-aft curvature of a keel or bottom of a vessel

rove: washer-like piece of metal forced over the point of a nail before it is clenched

rowlocks: a shaped space cut in a boat's gunwale to take an oar

run: to sail with the wind from the stern sector

running rigging: rigging used to hoist, lower or trim sails, or to hoist or strike the yards. See: standing rigging

scarf: tapered or wedge-shaped joint between pieces of similar section at the joint

sea breeze: wind that blows from sea to land during the day once the land temperature rises above that of the sea

seam: juncture of two members required to be watertight

settee: quadrilateral, lateen sail with a short leading edge

sheer/sheerline: curve of the upper edge of the hull

sheer strake: top strake of planking

sheet: line used to trim foot of a sail

shore: stout timber used to support hull of a vessel after she has taken the ground

shrouds: ropes leading from masthead to sides of vessel to support mast athwartships

shunted: specialised way of changing tack undertaken by an Oceanic single outrigger boat that has her mast stepped amidships;

after such a manoeuvre, the former stern becomes the bow

sided: dimension of a timber measured (near) parallel to the fore-and-aft plane (or the keel) of a vessel

side timber: framing timber supporting side planking at stations between <u>floor</u> timbers; may be adjacent to a floor but is not fastened to it

spile: transfer a curved line onto a pattern which, when laid flat, will give the shape to cut a timber or a plank

spline: a flexible strip of wood used to draw curves

sprit: four-sided, fore-and-aft sail set on a sprit (spar) the lower end of which is made fast to the mast, while its upper end supports the peak of the sail

square sail: four-sided sail, laced to a yard which generally lies square (at right angles) to the fore-an-aft line

stabilisers: external longitudinal timbers fastened to a boat's sides at the loaded waterline to increase transverse stability. A similar effect is caused by 'furring' – see: <u>girdling</u>

stanchion: a fixed, upright pillar supporting a vessel's deck

standing knee: a vertical <u>knee</u>, above the structural member supported

standing rigging: the fixed, permanent rigging supporting masts and yards

stays: ropes leading from masthead forward and aft to support mast

steerage way: a vessel has steerage way when sufficient water passes over her rudder for it to be used to steer

strake: a single <u>plank</u> or combination of planks stretching from bow to stern

stream: the horizontal movement (ebb and flow) of water as tides rise and fall

stringer: longitudinal strength member along inside of <u>planking</u>

swell: an undulation that the sea retains for some time after a storm has ceased or a high wind has dropped

tack: (i). lower forward corner of a fore-and-aft sail. (ii). to alter course so that the bow of a sailing vessel passes through the wind

tacking spar: a spar used to hold the weather leach of a square sail to the wind

tender: said of a vessel inclined to heel well-over in a moderate breeze

tenon: piece of wood, rectangular in cross section, used to join timbers. May be an integral part of one timber, or may be 'loose', or 'locked' by a trans-piercing <u>dowel</u>

thole: wooden pin projecting upwards at <u>sheer</u> level to provide a pivot for an oar

throat: upper, forward corner of a four-sided. fore-and-aft sail

thwart: transverse member (<u>crossbeam</u>) used as a seat

tidal range: difference between height of high water and the next low water

timber: generally, any piece of timber used in boatbuilding; one-piece <u>ribs</u>, especially those steamed or bent into shape, are known as 'timbers'

tradition: 'boatbuilding tradition' is a conceptual tool, an archaeological /historical construct used to increase understanding: a perceived style of boatbuilding used in a specified region during a given period

transition strake: <u>strake</u> at the transition between bottom and side of a boat, especially where there is a marked change in the boat's transverse section

transom: athwartship <u>bulkhead</u>, usually at the stern, occasionally at the bow

treenail: hardwood peg, of multi-faceted section, with a head at one end and (sometimes) a wedge at the other. Used to join two members

trireme: oared and sailed vessel with three levels of oarsmen

trux: the several wooden balls in a <u>parrel</u> that facilitate movement around, and up and down, the mast

turned nail: fastening nail clenched by turning the tip through 90° to lie along the face of the <u>timber</u>

tumblehome: inboard inclination of the upper sides of a vessel; opposite of 'flare'

GLOSSARY

volumetric coefficient: ratio of <u>displacement</u> to the cube of waterline length

voyage: journey made at sea, including both outward and homeward <u>passages</u>

wale: <u>strake</u> thicker than the others

washstrake: an additional <u>strake</u> fitted to increase <u>freeboard</u> and to keep out spray and water

wear: alter course by passing the stern of the sailing vessel through the wind

weather helm: a vessel is said to 'carry weather helm' when the tiller has to be kept to windward to counteract the vessel's tendency to come up into the wind

windlass: similar to a <u>capstan</u>, but on a horizontal shaft

yard: spar suspended from a mast and to which the head of a square sail is bent

yardarm: the ends of a <u>yard</u>, to which <u>braces</u> are made fast

zenith: highest point of a heavenly body's trajectory

Note: Underlined words within a definition refer to another entry in this glossary.

Index